THE DECLARATION OF SOMETHING *Mysterious*

Jesus' Courage and Communication of the Truth
A Study of Luke 10:38–16:18

BIBLE STUDY GUIDE

From the Bible-teaching ministry of

Charles R. Swindoll

Insight for Living

Chuck graduated in 1963 from Dallas Theological Seminary, where he now serves as the school's fourth president, helping to prepare a new generation of men and women for the ministry. Chuck has served in pastorates in three states: Massachusetts, Texas, and California, including almost twenty-three years at the First Evangelical Free Church in Fullerton, California. His sermon messages have been aired over radio since 1979 as the *Insight for Living* broadcast. A best-selling author, Chuck has written numerous books and booklets on many subjects.

Based on the outlines and transcripts of Chuck's sermons, the study guide text is coauthored by Bryce Klabunde, a graduate of Biola University and Dallas Theological Seminary. He also wrote the Living Insights sections.

Editor in Chief:
Cynthia Swindoll

Coauthor of Text:
Bryce Klabunde

Assistant Editor:
Wendy Peterson

Copy Editors:
Deborah Gibbs
Glenda Schlahta
Karene Wells

Text Designer:
Gary Lett

Publishing System Specialist:
Bob Haskins

Director, Communications and Marketing Division:
Deedee Snyder

Marketing Manager:
Alene Cooper

Project Coordinator:
Colette Muse

Production Manager:
John Norton

Printer:
Sinclair Printing Company

ISBN 0-8499-8624-9
COVER DESIGN: Gary Lett
COVER PAINTING: *The Sermon on the Mount* by Carl Bloch
The Granger Collection, New York
Printed in the United States of America

CONTENTS

INTRODUCTION

Words are powerful things. Who among us hasn't felt the impact of the right words said at just the right moment, in just the right way? Solomon described their value this way:

> Like apples of gold in settings of silver
> Is a word spoken in right circumstances.
> (Prov. 25:11)

No words have ever been more powerful than those our Lord Jesus Christ spoke while He was on this earth. His words held the rabbis of His day in rapt attention. His words nourished His disciples and kept them going after He was gone. His words stirred up the hostility of the Pharisees and the scribes, provoking them enough to haul Him into a Roman court. And it was His words, twisted and misrepresented, that the legalists used to nail His hands and feet to the cross.

As we move into the section of Luke from the end of chapter 10 to the middle of chapter 16, we will see Jesus' words playing a more up-front role in His ministry. His stories and parables, discourses and instructions will take more of the limelight than His actions.

Remember, in the end, Jesus will not be condemned for what He did—He will die for what He said.

So I encourage you to get to know the words of Jesus intimately. Read them. Test them. Master them. Let them settle in your mind and wrap themselves around your heart, for they are the words of eternal life.

Chuck Swindoll

Chuck Swindoll

Putting Truth into Action

Knowledge apart from application falls short of God's desire for His children. He wants us to apply what we learn so that we will change and grow. This study guide was prepared with these goals in mind. As you go through the following pages, we hope your desire to discover biblical truth will grow as your understanding of God's Word increases and that you will be encouraged to apply what you've learned.

To assist you in your study, we've included a section called **Living Insights** at the end of each lesson. These exercises will challenge you to study further and to think of specific ways to put your discoveries into action.

There are many ways to use this guide—in personal devotions, group studies, discussions with friends and family, and Sunday school classes. And, of course, it's an ideal study aid when you're listening to its corresponding *Insight for Living* radio series.

To benefit most from this study guide, we would encourage you to consider it a spiritual journal. That's why we've included space in the **Living Insights** for recording your thoughts and discoveries. We hope you'll return to those sections often for review and encouragement as you continue to grow in your walk with Christ.

Bryce Klabunde

Bryce Klabunde
Coauthor of Text
Author of Living Insights

THE DECLARATION OF SOMETHING *Mysterious*

Jesus' Courage and Communication of the Truth
A Study of Luke 10:38–16:18

LUKE: A PHYSICIAN'S OPINION

Writer: Luke, a Gentile Christian physician (first mentioned in Acts 16:10)

Date: Around A.D. 60

Style: Scholarly, detailed, people-oriented

Appeal: Directly to Greeks, but universal

Message: Jesus is truly human

Key Phrase: "The Son of Man" (Luke 19:10)

Interesting Facts:

- This is the only gospel account specifically addressed to an individual: "most excellent Theophilus" (friend of God). William Barclay calls Luke 1:1–4, "well-nigh the best Greek in the New Testament."[1]
- Luke records the first hints of Christian hymnology (1:46–55, 68–79; 2:14, 29–32).
- More pictures have been painted by artists who derive their inspiration from Luke than any other New Testament book.
- Between chapters 9 and 19 there are over 30 sayings, parables, and incidents mentioned nowhere else in Scripture.

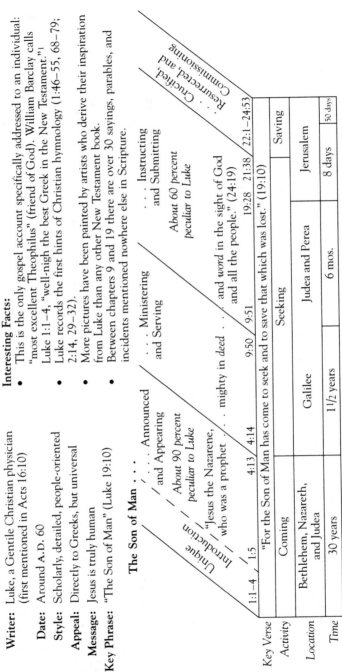

The Son of Man . . .

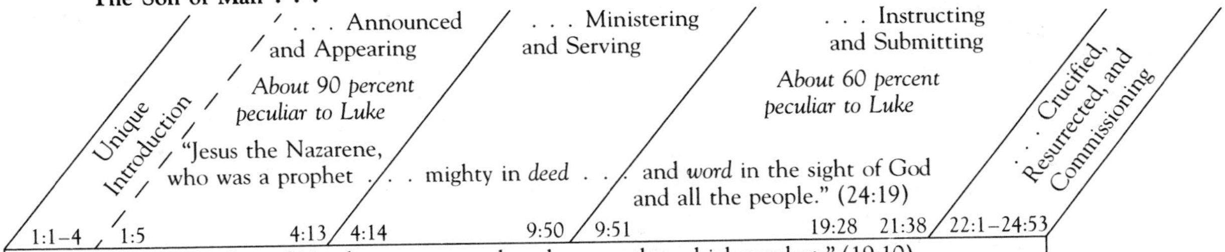

	1:5–4:13	4:14–9:50	9:51–19:28	19:28–21:38	22:1–24:53
Key Verse	"For the Son of Man has come to seek and to save that which was lost." (19:10)				
Activity	Coming	Seeking			Saving
Location	Bethlehem, Nazareth, and Judea	Galilee	Judea and Perea	Jerusalem	
Time	30 years	1½ years	6 mos.	8 days	50 days

1. William Barclay, *The Gospel of Luke*, rev. ed., The Daily Study Bible Series (Philiadelphia, Pa.: Westminster Press, 1975), p. 2.

Chapter 1

Taming the Lion within Us

Luke 10:38–42

The photographer steps around the tangle of cords and equipment in the studio, adjusting lights and arranging family members like fruit in a still life. "Tilt your head a little, Mom . . . that's good. Dad, chin up a bit. Kids, hands folded. Great. OK, everyone look at me and . . . *smile*."

Pop! The lights flash. The camera blinks. For a fraction of a second, everyone puts on their best face and the film records the perfect family portrait.

Once home from the studio, however, the true faces emerge as neckties loosen and carefully combed relationships frazzle. Mom and Dad speak curtly to one another. The teenager retreats under his headphones. And the younger ones resume their usual whining, poking, and tattling.

For the camera and the public we show one side of ourselves, but our home lives reveal the true image behind the glossy photos. If you want to know what a person is really like, you have to enter the home. That's where Scripture takes its camera. And the Bible doesn't airbrush its family portraits; it shows us the true picture.

A Few Familiar "Family Portraits" in Scripture

Take a look, for instance, at the Bible's portrait of Adam and Eve's family. Even the memories of Paradise can't smooth over the

Sections of this chapter have been adapted from "Christ at the Crossroad of Anxiety," in the study guide *Christ at the Crossroads*, coauthored by Lee Hough, from the Bible-teaching ministry of Charles R. Swindoll (Anaheim, Calif.: Insight for Living, 1991), pp. 20–26.

ugly image of Cain murdering his brother (Gen. 4:1–10). The picture of faithful Abraham and Sarah actually reveals glaring faithlessness as Sarah gives her handmaid to Abraham to bear the promised son (16:1–3). And who can miss the collage of tragedy in David's family? Images of adultery, rape, and rebellion fill the frame (2 Sam. 11–18).

It's easy to point fingers of judgment at these families. But what would our families look like in the revealing light of Scripture? Would we see brother against brother? A lack of faith? Rebellion? Envy?

With an attitude of self-examination, we come to one of the most personal and intimate family vignettes from Scripture, recorded by Luke in chapter 10 of his gospel.

An Unforgettable Scene in Bethany

For about two and a half years, Jesus has been on the road, ministering in village after village. The divine clock is ticking away His remaining six months on earth as He makes His final journey . . . toward Jerusalem, toward the Cross. Traveling with His disciples,

> He entered a certain village; and a woman named Martha welcomed Him into her home. (Luke 10:38)

The Place

The village is Bethany (see John 11:1), which is two miles from Jerusalem. Martha's sister, Mary, and her brother, Lazarus, also live here—although Lazarus will not appear in the story. Their home is a place where Jesus knows He can find a refuge among special friends who won't demand miracles or ask leading questions. It's a home where He knows He is loved and accepted, where He knows He can rest.

The People

Home is not merely a place; it's people. In *Intimate Moments with the Savior*, author Ken Gire takes us inside the door with Jesus and introduces the two sisters.

> Martha, so eager to serve. Energetic. First to roll up her sleeves and pitch in to help. Last to leave until every dish is cleaned and put away. Up early. First at the market. Haggles to get the best prices. To the point, sometimes even abrupt. The yolks of the eggs

she serves for breakfast are never broken. The fruit she sets out in a wooden bowl on the table is always fresh and sweet. Dinner is never overcooked. The perfect hostess.

And Mary? Well, she's up about thirty minutes later. Sometimes goes with her sister to the market, but more often than not, doesn't. The haggling bothers her. Likes to cook, but doesn't like to clean up the mess. Perceptive. Asks few but thoughtful questions. Is a good listener. Sensitive and calm.[1]

Both sisters are delighted to see Jesus. How they express their enthusiasm, however, is very different.

The Disagreement

Luke first tells us about Mary.

> And she had a sister called Mary, who moreover was listening to the Lord's word, seated at His feet. (Luke 10:39)

Mary is focused; she clears her mind of all the incidentals and makes room for the essential—Jesus. She is content to listen, to be with Christ and not "do" anything. And Martha?

> But Martha was distracted with all her preparations. (v. 40a)

Mary sees Jesus and thinks, *The Savior!* Martha sees Him and thinks, *I must prepare a meal!*

At this point, preachers often give Martha a sound pulpit pounding for her response. But, honestly, would we have reacted much differently? We all know what unplanned visits are like. And if the disciples are with Jesus too, no wonder Martha is flustered.

The problem isn't her natural reaction to the situation as much as her placing her own agenda over Christ's. Knowing His time is short, Jesus is hoping for a satisfying taste of warm, quiet fellowship. An elaborate meal with all the trimmings is Martha's idea. She pays too much attention to the things that don't matter and not enough to the things that do.

1. Ken Gire, *Intimate Moments with the Savior* (Grand Rapids, Mich.: Zondervan Publishing House, 1989), p. 64.

From the moment Christ came in the door, she has been distracted with the incidentals connected with being the perfect hostess. She is busy—too busy. And it isn't long before those incidentals begin grating on her. Take a good look at Martha working in her kitchen, where more than just the oven is heating up.

> *I can't believe Mary isn't in here helping*, she thinks. Martha pushes a fist into the dough. *She should be in here*. Another fist into the dough. *We could get this done in half the time*. She pulls and mashes, pulls and mashes. *You know, I'd like to hear what he has to say, too, but somebody's got to fix dinner*. Martha reaches for some flour and flings it on the lump. *They could at least come in here while they talk*. She works the flour into the expanding loaf. *I can't believe he just lets her sit there*. Another fist into the dough. *Here I am in the kitchen, sweating, working my fingers to the bone . . . doesn't he care?*[2]

Martha's hot and getting hotter, until her anger explodes and she comes boiling out of the kitchen, red-faced and furious.

> "Lord, do You not care that my sister has left me to do all the serving alone? Then tell her to help me." (v. 40b)

She doesn't even call Mary by name. Through clenched teeth, she says, "my sister," and accuses her of shirking. Unthinkingly, she also takes a stab at Jesus, accusing Him—the Savior bound for the Cross—of lacking concern.

Martha's rash response illustrates what happens when the peculiarities of our temperament get the best of us. Authors Gary Smalley and John Trent describe four common temperaments in terms of animals. People who are Lions are "strong, aggressive, take-charge types." Playful Otters are "energetic, fun-loving souls." Golden Retrievers are "loyal, supportive, nurturing encouragers." And hard-working Beavers are "detail-oriented, careful, methodic, and thorough to a fault."[3]

2. Gire, *Intimate Moments with the Savior*, p. 66.

3. Gary Smalley and John Trent, *Home Remedies: Timeless Prescriptions for Today's Family* (Portland, Oreg.: Multnomah, 1991), pp. 79, 81, 84, 86.

A classic Golden Retriever, Mary tuned in to Jesus and was unaware of practical matters, like eating. Half Lion and half Beaver, Martha couldn't sit down and enjoy talking until she had checked off all the items on her to-do list. We owe a lot to the Marthas of the world. Without them, nothing would ever get done. But in this case, Martha's strengths had become her liabilities. Her Beaver and Lion traits had turned into badger and wolverine!

The Response

Jesus tames Martha's over-aggressive Lion with a stroke of His hand and a calm, reassuring word. "Martha, Martha," He says tenderly, cooling her anger with affection.

> "You are worried and bothered about so many things; but only a few things are necessary, really only one, for Mary has chosen the good part, which shall not be taken away from her." (vv. 41–42)

He does care about her, more than she realizes. He understands her temperament and wants to help her see beyond the momentary tension and embarrassment to the real issue. Fretting about the meal is robbing Martha of life's true joy—fellowship with Christ. The Son of God, who has precious little time left, is sitting in her living room. And she has chosen to bake bread, set the table, preparepreparepreprepare, instead of enjoy her Savior.

Do you see yourself in this family portrait? Do "so many things" distract you from the one necessary thing? Do Marys and Marthas clash in your home? Is your house a flurry of activity with little time for essentials?

Some Convicting Observations

No family is perfect. Behind our public smiles are private battles that rage within us and between us. We all have a tendency to be Lions, roaring in anger, sinking teethlike accusations into people, pouncing on others for not doing what we want them to do.

If you've been on the prowl lately, ask yourself a couple of questions: "Is anything distracting me from focusing on Christ? Are any nonessentials worrying and bothering me to the point of frustration and anger?" If so, let Mary and Martha's story teach you three things.

First, *when facing a test, it's easy to let our temperament dictate the agenda*. Take-charge Martha thought she knew what Jesus wanted and set out to do it, not even bothering to ask whether He wanted something entirely different. If you're like that, take time to listen first, then act.

Second, *when life gets complicated, it's helpful to remember that simplicity is the best policy*. Jesus' needs were simple—a place to rest, a cup of water, and someone to share it with. Many times, that's all we need too.

Third, *when time is critical, it is essential to focus on the eternal rather than the temporal*. Our world is full of distractions. And the more the pressure, the more tempting it is to focus on the urgent rather than the essential. Don't let a fast-paced life rob you of the quiet joy of communion with Christ. Be like Mary, who made her bread from the "good part" of life (v. 42). Her food would satisfy her forever.

Living Insights — STUDY ONE

Has anyone ever been able to prepare an ideal, Norman Rockwell Thanksgiving dinner? Personally, I don't think it can be done. Yet, every year, millions of us swarm the markets intent on perfection. We contemplate the turkeys. Fresh or frozen? Sniff the sweet potatoes. Snap the beans. We want only the best ingredients for our stuffings and salads and pies.

When "T-Day" arrives, we're up before dawn. There's so much to do—braising and basting, mashing and mincing, peeling and pounding. Loiterers in the kitchen, beware!

With oven and stove blazing, we perfectly synchronize each dish to emerge at the same time and piping hot. Setting out our finest china, we transform our humble dining room table into a work of art, ready to receive the bountiful spread.

Then the inevitable happens. After the family gives thanks, someone spoons to death our luscious salad. Another attacks our whipped potatoes. And another stabs our beautiful golden turkey and slices it to the bone.

In less than a half-hour, a masterpiece meal that took days to create has turned into leftovers and a pile of dirty dishes.

Suddenly, it occurs to us that the day has flown by, and the only words we've spoken to anyone have been, "Don't touch that," and, "Out of the kitchen, all of you!" As we survey the carnage, we think, *Maybe a perfect meal wasn't the most important thing today.*

Striving for perfection is an admirable trait. But it's also a trait destined to distract. Like Martha, we can become worried and bothered over so many things that we miss the truly important things, namely our relationships with others and with Christ.

Take a moment to look within. Where is your focus? Have you been giving yourself to nonessentials—things that will be here today and tossed out tomorrow? What has been most important to you lately?

What needs to be more important to you?

How can you begin to value those things that matter most?

Living Insights — STUDY TWO

"I worked myself to the bone, and this is the thanks I get?" We can almost hear Martha grumbling under her breath at Mary and Jesus. Well, shouldn't they have been more appreciative for all that she was doing? After all, she was only trying to serve.

No one faults her for her intentions. Jesus deserved the best, and the best was what she wanted to give Him. The problem was, she never asked Jesus what He preferred.

Commentator William Barclay makes an astute observation about Martha's misguided act of kindness.

> Here is one of the great difficulties in life. So often we want to be kind to people—but we want to be kind to them *in our way;* and should it happen that our way is not the necessary way, we sometimes take offence and think that we are not appreciated. If we are trying to be kind the first necessity is to try to see into the heart of the person we desire to help—and then to forget all our own plans and to think only of what he or she needs.[4]

If you're planning a gift or an act of kindness, take a minute to think through what your friend or relative really needs. In the following space, work out the details of what you'd like to do for them. Scrap your original ideas if necessary, and come up with just the right gift.

____

____

____

____

____

It's true, giving has its own rewards. But the best rewards come when the giver truly has the other person's best interests in mind.

4. William Barclay, *The Gospel of Luke*, rev. ed., The Daily Study Bible Series (Philadelphia, Pa.: Westminster Press, 1975), p. 142.

Chapter 2

LORD, TEACH US TO PRAY

Luke 11:1–13

I can read your mind. Don't believe me? I'll prove it to you.

Pick a number between 1 and 10, and write it in this space.	
Multiply your number by 9.	
If you have a number with two digits, add the first and the second digits together and write the number in this space. (If your number is a single digit, just write that number down.)	
Subtract 5 from your number.	
Pick the letter of the alphabet that corresponds with your number (*A* is 1, *B* is 2, etc.). Write your letter in this space.	
Next, write down the letter of the alphabet that immediately follows your letter.	
You now have two letters. Write down the name of a country that begins with your first letter and the name of an animal that begins with your second letter.	

Of all the countries and animals in the world, do you think I can guess which ones you wrote down? To find out, turn to the end of this lesson (page 14) for my answer.

Was I right? Pretty amazing, huh! Actually, it's just a matter of math and odds. The chances were good that you would write down what you did.

Now let's see if I can read your mind again. Imagine this situation. It's late at night and you're driving through an unfamiliar part of town. Suddenly, your tire blows, and you thump, thump, thump to the side of the road . . . and you remember that your spare is flat too. What do you do first?

Probably, you would pray. Most of us would. We all believe in prayer when our backs are against a wall and we're in danger. But what about other times, when the sun is shining and we're cruising through life carefree? What are the odds that we would be praying as fervently then?

Admission: Things on Which We Agree

Though most Christians would agree that prayer is powerful and that God honors moment-by-moment communion with Him, we still struggle to make it a central part of our daily lives. At some point in our Christian walk, we'd all have to admit:

1. We don't pray as we should (see James 4:2b)—not as quickly, not as often, not as specifically, not as confidently.
2. We lack the power and relief prayer could bring (compare Phil. 4:6–7)—instead, fear and worry tie our insides in knots.
3. We need help to change this habit of prayerlessness—we can't do it on our own.

Fortunately, we are not left to ourselves. No one is better able or more willing to teach us about prayer than Jesus Himself.

Instruction: Guidelines We Should Follow

The disciples felt a similar void in their lives. And like hungry children, they came to the Lord asking for a taste of the spiritual food that kept Him so well-nourished and satisfied.

> And it came about that while He was praying in a certain place, after He had finished, one of His disciples said to Him, "Lord, teach us to pray just as John also taught his disciples." (Luke 11:1)

Where would Jesus go, and what would He pray about? Perhaps, on a mountainside or along a quiet stream, somewhere away from the pressing crowd, He talked with the Father about the Cross or His concerns for His followers. Or maybe He just sank down beside his bed at night and asked for the strength to go on. Wherever He was, whatever His topic, the disciples were watching. And they wanted to do it too.

Prayer, like many aspects of our walk with God, does not come naturally; it must be taught.

So, without hesitation, Jesus ushered the disciples into His spiritual storehouse and offered them the truth they hungrily sought. Two basic elements emerge from the prayer Jesus modeled.[1] The first, in verse 2, concerns our relationship with God. The second, in verses 3–4, centers on our personal requests.

Reverence for Our Heavenly Father

> And He said to them, "When you pray, say:
> 'Father, hallowed be Thy name.
> Thy kingdom come.'" (v. 2)

Right at the start, Jesus shows us the ground on which we stand before God. He doesn't tell us to call Him "Friend," as though we were equal with Him. Or "Master," as though we were slaves. Or "King," as though we were one of the masses. Our relationship with God is that of child to parent.

As our Father, He gives us life. He cares for us and helps us grow to maturity. He knows us better than we know ourselves, and He longs to give us what is best for us. Because we are His children, we have permission to come into His celestial "office" any time we want—even on one of His busiest days—climb in His lap, and talk to Him.

Do you find it difficult to picture such a good and kind, involved and caring father? Perhaps your dad was an angry, unapproachable, or abusive man. God understands what a hindrance this is in your life. Maybe one way to begin overcoming it is to think of God as being everything you may have wished for in a father. All the dreams you've had of a loving, wise, and decent dad can be realized in your heavenly Father—and so much more.

The next phrase, "hallowed be Thy name," shows the attitude we are to show toward God. The word *hallow* conveys two ideas:

> 1: to make holy or set apart for holy use, 2: to respect greatly.[2]

When we walk across the Civil War battlefield at Gettysburg

1. Luke's version of the Lord's Prayer is shorter than the more familiar version in Matthew 6:9–13. Some scholars attribute the variation to Jesus probably having taught this prayer to the disciples more than once. And since it was meant to be a model, not a rigid formula, it makes sense that it would vary. See Leon Morris, *The Gospel according to St. Luke*, The Tyndale New Testament Commentaries Series (Grand Rapids, Mich.: William B. Eerdmans Publishing Co., 1974), p. 192.

2. *Webster's Collegiate Dictionary*, 10th ed., see "hallow."

or overlook the war cemetery at Normandy, a sense of respectful awe hushes our spirits. This is hallowed ground. We wouldn't think of setting up a carnival here or leveling it to construct a shopping mall. In a similar way, when we approach our heavenly Father, we are approaching a hallowed Person. We must come holding His name in highest regard. We must keep in mind whom we're talking to—the Father, yes, but also the holy Sovereign of the universe, who has a glorious plan for His creation.

By praying, "Thy kingdom come," we acknowledge that His plan for the world and for our lives surpasses our own plans. And because both His name and His authority are supreme, we come glorifying His name and submitting ourselves to His kingdom agenda. This is the perspective Jesus wants us to have toward God when we pray.

Requests for Our Needs

> "'Give us each day our daily bread.
> And forgive us our sins,
> For we ourselves also forgive everyone who is
> indebted to us.
> And lead us not into temptation.'" (vv. 3–4)

With this next section of His prayer, Jesus gives us permission to be practical. We don't have to write our requests in the clouds with lofty-minded supplications. We can bring them down to earth. In these verses, Jesus addresses three of our most basic needs.

First, He considers our need for "daily bread," that is, our physical necessities—food, clothing, shelter. The Father wants us to depend on Him each day for life's essentials.

Second, He addresses our need for daily spiritual cleansing. What food is to the body, forgiveness is to the soul. To receive cleansing of sins, we must simply ask for it. But our appeal must well up from a soft and repentant heart, one that is willing to give as well as receive forgiveness.

Third, He speaks of our need for daily purity. By teaching us to pray, "Lead us not into temptation," Jesus wasn't implying that God is the one who tempts us. James states that God "does not tempt anyone" (James 1:13). The idea of the prayer is this: "Do not allow us to be led into temptation." It's a prayer for God's protection from Satan's insidious traps. Each day, Jesus is saying, pray that the Lord will remind you of your vulnerable areas, guard your eyes, guide your thoughts, and keep you pure.

Admonition: Techniques We Should Remember

Having provided some guidelines for us in His model prayer, Jesus next fills in some details with a couple of techniques.

Don't Let Up . . . Persist!

First, He encourages us to be persistent when we pray.

> And He said to them, "Suppose one of you shall have a friend, and shall go to him at midnight, and say to him, 'Friend, lend me three loaves; for a friend of mine has come to me from a journey, and I have nothing to set before him'; and from inside he shall answer and say, 'Do not bother me; the door has already been shut and my children and I are in bed; I cannot get up and give you anything.' I tell you, even though he will not get up and give him anything because he is his friend, yet because of his persistence he will get up and give him as much as he needs. And I say to you, ask, and it shall be given to you; seek, and you shall find; knock, and it shall be opened to you. For everyone who asks, receives; and he who seeks, finds; and to him who knocks, it shall be opened." (Luke 11:5–10)

The midnight visitor received the bread he needed because he kept on knocking. The Greek word for *persistence* literally means "shamelessness." He wasn't concerned about social graces. He didn't care if he wakened the whole neighborhood. He needed bread, and he shamelessly persisted until he received it.

Do we approach God with that same kind of bold endurance? Or do we knock one time, hear nothing, and quietly tiptoe away? Jesus is saying, "Keep asking, keep seeking, keep knocking!"

Don't Doubt . . . Trust!

And at the same time, "Keep trusting."

> "Now suppose one of you fathers is asked by his son for a fish; he will not give him a snake instead of a fish, will he? Or if he is asked for an egg, he will not give him a scorpion, will he? If you then, being evil,

> know how to give good gifts to your children, how much more shall your heavenly Father give the Holy Spirit to those who ask Him?" (vv. 11–13)

If we trust our earthly fathers to give us good gifts, we can certainly trust our heavenly Father to provide for our needs. He even goes beyond what we ask and gives us His Holy Spirit, who guides us during times of waiting and comforts us in times of pain.

Clarification: When It Comes to Prayer

Do you want to pray like Jesus? Here's a summary of His simple method. Talk to God as to a loving father. Approach Him with an attitude of awe and respect. Submit to His kingdom plan. Bring Him your requests daily. Depend on Him for everything—the necessities of life, spiritual cleansing, purity. Don't forget to be persistent. And, whatever you do, keep on trusting.

Prayer isn't as complicated as we sometimes make it. Jesus has given some helpful advice that all of us can follow. As we do, let's remember a couple of things. First, we can count on God to answer clearly. Maybe not quickly and maybe not with a yes. But, as time passes, we can look back and see His answer unfold.

Also, we must never hesitate to be bold. Do we truly believe in prayer? Do we truly believe in a good and kind heavenly Father? Then we need to keep on asking. Keep on seeking. Keep on knocking. Persistence is the key that opens the gates of heaven.

Answers to the Mind-Reading Test: Denmark, elephant. (No matter which number between 1 and 10 you choose and multiply by 9, the sum of the digits will always total 9. So the letters will always be the fourth and fifth, or D and E, and more often than not people will think of *Denmark* and *elephant* first.)

Living Insights STUDY ONE

A mutual fund brings the highest dividends when we invest in it steadily over a long period of time. Similarly, we see the greatest return on our prayers when we invest in them consistently, day after day, month after month, year after year.

Have you stopped making deposits lately? Sometimes we get so busy we forget. Or we see little payoff, so we give up hope. If God issued a fund statement on your prayer life, would it show steady growth, stops and starts, or a dwindling account?

Is there someone or something you need to start praying for regularly?

Tape this request to your refrigerator, your telephone, your bathroom mirror. Place it so that you can't go through the day without being reminded to pray. Will your investment pay off? Charles Spurgeon answers with an enthusiastic *yes!*

> If there be anything I know, anything that I am quite assured of beyond all question, it is that praying breath is never spent in vain.[3]

Living Insights STUDY TWO

Jesus teaches us that prayer consists of both the dust of humanity and the air of eternity. It is both earthly and heavenly, ordinary and extraordinary. It is as casual as picking up the telephone and as terrifying as realizing God is on the other end.

For that reason, Eugene Peterson calls prayer "a daring venture into speech." He writes,

> When we venture into prayer, every word may, at any moment, come to mean just what it *means* and involve us with a holy God who wills our holiness. All we had counted on was some religious small talk,

3. Charles Spurgeon, as quoted in *Spurgeon at His Best,* comp. Tom Carter (Grand Rapids, Mich.: Baker Book House, 1988), p. 142.

> a little numinous gossip, and we are suddenly involved, without intending it and without having calculated the consequences, in something *eternal*.[4]

Are you prepared to enter into this eternal, dangerous venture called prayer? When you say, "Father, hallowed be Thy name," are you ready for the personal changes a holy God may bring? When you say, "Thy kingdom come," do you truly desire His kingdom plan to break forth in your life?

Peterson warns,

> We want life on our conditions, not on God's conditions. Praying puts us at risk of getting involved in God's conditions.[5]

Are you willing to take the risk?

Use the following space to pour out your desire to the Lord. Let Him know that you want your prayer life not only to change things but also to change you.

____

____

____

____

____

____

____

4. Eugene H. Peterson, *Working the Angles: The Shape of Pastoral Integrity* (Grand Rapids, Mich.: William B. Eerdmans Publishing Co., 1987), p. 43.

5. Peterson, *Working the Angles*, p. 44.

Chapter 3

STORMING HELLISH GATES

Luke 11:14–26

All sorts of lenses help us get a better look at our world. Microscopic cameras invite doctors to peer into the inner workings of our bodies, while gigantic telescopes let astronomers keep an eye on vast, unreachable galaxies. We've sure come a long way since Benjamin Franklin's first pair of bifocals! Yet no matter how advanced our technology becomes, no lens will ever bring into focus the invisible world of spirits.

If only we could peek beyond the haze of our earthly atmosphere into the realm of angels. What incredible sights we would see! Legions of mighty beings moving across the sky, skirmishes between the forces of light and darkness, a never-ending battle taking place right beside us.

We may never get a glimpse of this spiritual conflict, yet the battle does exist. Paul says that

> our struggle is not against flesh and blood, but against the rulers, against the powers, against the world forces of this darkness, against the spiritual forces of wickedness in the heavenly places. (Eph. 6:12)

You've probably sensed the struggle—though you may not have realized it at the time. For instance, have you ever tried to understand biblical truth and felt blocked? Or been unable to get certain self-destructive thoughts off your mind? Or had shameful images keep playing over and over on your mental screen? These are spiritual battles, and they rage all around us. Constantly. Unrelentingly. Viciously.

While on earth, Jesus drew our demonic foes into the open so we could get a good look at their hideous nature. In this chapter, we'll see Him encounter and defeat an evil spirit. Then, from His example, we'll map out battle strategies for our own fight with the Enemy.

Gaining an Understanding of Opposing Forces

To help us better understand this war, let's gather some intelligence on the opposing forces—the kingdom of light and the kingdom of darkness.

	The Kingdom of Light	*The Kingdom of Darkness*
Ultimate Authority	The Living God (God the Father)	The Devil (Satan, Lucifer, Son of the Morning, Angel of Light, Beelzebul)
Ultimate Destination	Heaven, the place of eternal bliss with God	Hell, the place of unending torment and everlasting punishment
Strategy	Redemption through the grace of the Cross	Deception through hidden, wicked schemes
Ultimate Outcome	Wins	Loses

Defeated at the Cross, the Devil has only one recourse left in his losing battle—to drag as many people as he can down with him. He shuts people's ears to the gospel. He sabotages the church and undermines our witness. He would destroy us altogether, except that Jesus has promised, "I will build My church; and the gates of Hades shall not overpower it" (Matt. 16:18).

Never forget that Christ is on our side. With just a word, He makes demons tremble and drives them away whimpering—like in the following situation, in which Jesus encountered a demon living in a man who could not speak.

Dealing with the Powers of Darkness

Trapped in a voiceless torment, unable even to cry out for help, a demonized man suddenly gains freedom at Jesus' strong, merciful hands.

Casting Out a Demon

> And He was casting out a demon, and it was dumb; and it came about that when the demon had gone out, the dumb man spoke; and the multitudes marveled. (Luke 11:14)

Can you imagine not being able to call a warning to a child in danger or vocalize your deepest feelings? That was this man's *life*. Yet when Jesus came near, the man didn't need words. The Lord heard the cry of his heart and immediately came to his rescue.

What sweet release was his! Jesus had snapped the chains of this man's demonic agony, and his thoughts and voice were his own again. No wonder the multitudes marveled.

Demons, you see, would have us believe they're all-powerful. But the truth is, they *must* obey the authority of Christ (see Luke 10:17; 1 John 4:4). And when Jesus' power drives them out, how blessed is the person's relief.

Set on the path of life, the liberated man must have overflowed with praise and gratitude. The scene shimmered with seamless joy—until the razor-sharp voices of Jesus' critics cut in.[1]

> But some of them said, "He casts out demons by Beelzebul,[2] the ruler of the demons." And others, to test Him, were demanding of Him a sign from heaven. (Luke 11:15–16)

Jesus had stepped into the cesspool of the demonic world to rescue the man, while from a safe distance His enemies had the gall to accuse Him of coming from that very sewer. "Show us a sign from heaven," they grumbled, "not from the pit."

Their guilt-by-association argument had one major flaw, however, which Jesus quickly exposed.

> But He knew their thoughts, and said to them, "Any kingdom divided against itself is laid waste; and a house divided against itself falls. And if Satan also is divided against himself, how shall his kingdom stand? For you say that I cast out demons by Beelzebul. And if I by Beelzebul cast out demons, by whom do your sons cast them out? Consequently they shall be your judges. But if I cast out demons by the finger of God, then the kingdom of God has come upon you." (vv. 17–20)

Since Satan wants to enslave people, not free them, he would be fighting against himself if he cast out his own demonic henchmen.

1. Matthew tells us these antagonists were the Pharisees (12:24).

2. Also rendered Baal-zebub, the god of Ekron (2 Kings 1), this name means "lord of flies." "Our best understanding . . . seems to be that the Jews took this name of a heathen god and understood it in terms of the similar sounding Hebrew [Baalzebul], 'lord of dung.' They applied it to a prominent demon, perhaps to Satan himself. Jesus clearly understood it as referring to Satan." Leon Morris, *The Gospel according to St. Luke*, The Tyndale New Testament Commentaries Series (Grand Rapids, Mich.: William B. Eerdmans Publishing Co., 1974), p. 197.

And if Jesus were following the Devil's orders—what about the other Jews who performed exorcisms? Were they servants of Beelzebul too?

If Jesus wasn't of Satan, then only one alternative remained: He must be of God. And if He cast out demons "by the finger of God," then God's kingdom was present as He had announced. What clearer sign of His Messiahship could the Jewish leaders want?

Discussion of the Demonic

Jesus' offer of His kingdom was the star around which His entire ministry revolved. He didn't care about simply winning an argument; He cared about winning lives. He longed to drive His point into the people's hearts.

> "When a strong man, fully armed, guards his own homestead, his possessions are undisturbed; but when someone stronger than he attacks him and overpowers him, he takes away from him all his armor on which he had relied, and distributes his plunder." (vv. 21–22)

The armed "strong man" is the Devil, who stakes his claim in a person's life. Christ, "someone stronger," overpowers the strong man, assumes his command, and distributes his plunder.[3] So who is greater? Who is worthy of our allegiance? Surely the conqueror — Christ.

Jesus climaxes His point in verse 23:

> "He who is not with Me is against Me; and he who does not gather with Me, scatters."

We are either for Him or against Him. We either gather or scatter, do good or do harm to His cause. We can't publicly pledge allegiance to His kingdom of light and privately make alliances with Satan's kingdom of darkness. There is no middle ground.

And it's not enough to merely clean up our behavior. A person can tidy up his or her life, yet neglect to put Christ at the center—which, as Jesus warns, can lead to frightening results.

3. Jesus' healing of the demoniac in Luke 8 is an example of distributing Satan's plunder. After freeing the man, Jesus encouraged him to "distribute" his life (which had been Satan's plunder) to others by testifying to the whole city what had happened to him (v. 39).

> "When the unclean spirit goes out of a man, it passes through waterless places seeking rest, and not finding any, it says, 'I will return to my house from which I came.' And when it comes, it finds it swept and put in order. Then it goes and takes along seven other spirits more evil than itself, and they go in and live there; and the last state of that man becomes worse than the first." (vv. 24–26)

What exactly is Jesus telling us? First, unclean spirits prefer to inhabit human bodies rather than to wander aimlessly through the netherworld ("waterless places"). Second, a life that is clean but without Christ is still helpless against the Adversary: it has no armor of God, no prayer, no protective presence of Christ. Third, a subsequent demonic encounter can be worse than the original one.

We can't trifle with demons. Mere intellect or will power have no effect on them. They will not be shaken free apart from Christ's intervention.

Facing the Adversary Today

Jesus doesn't explain this to frighten us but to prepare us. The simple truth is this: without Christ, we have no hope. But *with Him*, we can win the invisible war. Three vital strategies for victory come to the forefront as we reflect on this passage.

First, to understand Satan's strategy, we need information—we need *the Word of God*. The Bible is our CIA handbook, decoding our Enemy's schemes to help us plot his defeat. So before scrambling through a library or bookstore to do reconnaissance on spiritual warfare, first go to the Book.

Second, to withstand Enemy attacks, we need protection—we need *the armor of God*. Paul lists our equipment as truth, righteousness, the gospel, faith, salvation, the Word, and prayer (see Eph. 6:13–18). By donning this armor and wielding these spiritual weapons, we can effectively defend ourselves against the Devil's deadliest arrows.

Third, to be protected from demonic infiltration, we need salvation—we need *the gift of God*. Do you long for spiritual relief? Have you ever received the gift of forgiveness Christ bought for you on the Cross? Jesus is your only hope of freedom from Satan's power and the hold of sin. As Scripture tells us:

> "There is salvation in no one else; for there is no

> other name under heaven that has been given among men, by which we must be saved." (Acts 4:12)

Acknowledge your need for Christ right now, won't you? He is waiting for you with outstretched hands.

Living Insights STUDY ONE

When we trust Christ for our salvation, God immediately delivers us "from the domain of darkness" and transfers us "to the kingdom of His beloved Son" (Col. 1:13). He makes us alive with Christ, forgives "all our transgressions," and cancels out "the certificate of debt consisting of decrees against us" (2:13–14). What a wonderful gift! But there's even more. From the following verses, what else does God do for us when we become Christians?

Romans 8:15–17

1 Corinthians 6:19–20

Ephesians 2:5–6

In light of our position in Christ, does Satan have any authority over us (see Col. 2:15)?

The Devil may roar (1 Pet. 5:8), but can he harm us or take away anything God has given? What has the Lord promised us concerning our Enemy's attacks (see 2 Thess. 3:3)?

Now that we're more aware of our power in Christ, let's explore the Enemy's schemes in the next Living Insight so that "no advantage be taken of us by Satan" (2 Cor. 2:11).

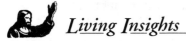

Living Insights STUDY TWO

In his book *The Bondage Breaker,* Neil Anderson describes three of Satan's strategies.

> How do these evil spirits interfere with our lives? Let me answer with a simple illustration. Imagine that you are standing at one end of a long, narrow street lined on both sides with two-story row houses. At the other end of the street stands Jesus Christ, and your Christian life is the process of walking down that long street of maturity in Him. . . .
>
> . . . Since this world is still under the dominion of Satan, the row houses on either side of you are inhabited by beings who are committed to keeping you from reaching your goal. They have no power or authority to block your path or even slow your step, so they hang out of the windows and call to you, hoping to turn your attention away from your goal and disrupt your progress.
>
> One of the ways they will try to distract you is by calling out, "Hey, look over here! I've got something you really want. It tastes good, feels good, and is a lot more fun than your boring walk down the street. Come on in and take a look." That's temptation, suggesting to your mind ways to serve yourself instead of God. . . .
>
> As you continue your walk toward Christ you will also have thoughts like "I'm stupid. I'm ugly. I'll never amount to anything for God." . . . Accusation is one of Satan's primary weapons in his attempt to distract you from your goal. . . .
>
> Other remarks which are hurled at you as you walk down the street sound like this: "You don't need to go to church today. It's not important to pray and read the Bible every day. Some of the New Age stuff isn't so bad." That's deception, and it is

> Satan's most subtle and debilitating weapon. You will often hear these messages in first-person singular: "I don't need to go to church today, pray, read my Bible," etc. Satan knows you will be more easily deceived if he can make you think the thought was yours instead of his.[4]

Once you can sense Satan's temptations, accusations, and subtle deceptions, you can expose them for what they are—frauds. Don't let them control your life. James says, "Resist the devil and he will flee from you" (4:7b). You don't need to be afraid of Satan, with Christ at your side.

4. Neil T. Anderson, *The Bondage Breaker* (Eugene, Oreg.: Harvest House Publishers, 1990), pp. 105–6.

Chapter 4

How Jesus Handled Compliments and Crowds

Luke 11:27–36

Leadership is hazardous work. Unexpected criticism falls from nowhere. Self-doubt and discouragement trigger emotional cave-ins. And pride, the most dangerous peril, sucks us under before we even realize we've been standing in its quicksand.

Author Eugene Peterson lets us know what happens when we stumble into that third pitfall, pride.

> We who regularly speak in the name of God to the people around us easily slip into speaking in godlike tones and assuming a godlike posture. The moment we do that, even slightly, any deference to us or defiance of us can lead us into taking on a god-identity. We are, after all, speaking God's word. When people praise us, there is something God-honoring in what they say. When people reject us, there is something God-defying in the way they act. In either case our vocational identification with God's cause and God's word make us vulnerable to mistaken god-identities.[1]

Anyone who has achieved a position of spiritual influence—whether pastor or layperson, whether at home or in the church, whether at work or in the community—is at risk. Gaining a following may have its blessings, but it surely has its liabilities as well.

The Blessings and Liabilities of Gaining a Following

Let's look at a few pros and cons of gaining a following as a spiritual leader. It might help in our own ministries, and it will help us better understand what Jesus faced as we continue to study His years of ministering here on earth.

1. Eugene H. Peterson, *Under the Unpredictable Plant* (Grand Rapids, Mich.: William B. Eerdmans Publishing Co., 1992), p. 85.

Pros	*Cons*
Large numbers of people receive biblical help and encouragement, which is deeply gratifying.	Leaders can become enamored with their own success. The focus shifts from the message to the messenger.
The truth of God spreads far and wide, bringing revival and renewal.	Popularity can produce an unsound, cult-like environment.
Loyal followers and praying disciples protect leaders from that which could discourage and distract.	Leaders can grow isolated and unaccountable, as they convince themselves of their own indispensability.

Success can be the answer to our prayers, but it can also snap our spiritual moorings, pull us away from God, and eventually sink our ministries. Yet, if we follow Christ's example, these hazards don't have to happen. Let's look, then, at Luke 11 and see how Jesus handled two aspects of success that put any leader at risk: compliments and crowds.

An Analysis of Jesus with His Large Group of Followers

Having vanquished a demon and prevailed over critics who accused Him of being empowered "by Beelzebul" (Luke 11:15), Jesus certainly had a rapt crowd to teach God's truths to. One woman in particular, impacted by His wisdom and depth of character, couldn't contain her enthusiasm. Praise burst out of her heart, drowning out His voice and the very teaching she loved. What's a teacher to do?

How He Handled a Compliment

> And it came about while He said these things, one of the women in the crowd raised her voice, and said to Him, "Blessed is the womb that bore You, and the breasts at which You nursed." But He said, "On the contrary, blessed are those who hear the word of God, and observe it." (Luke 11:27–28)

The woman spoke out of place, but can we fault her? It takes courage to say what's on our hearts to someone we admire. She meant well, and Jesus didn't fault her either. Instead, He broadened her misdirected praise into an instructive principle: The truly blessed are those who hear His words and choose of their own accord to obey them.

Jesus' gentle honesty teaches us to receive compliments carefully and humbly. A simple "thank you" is usually appropriate. But, whenever possible, we should try to expand the compliment to include others. Humble leaders know that many people deserve the credit, not just themselves.

Also, remember what Jesus said earlier: "Woe to you when all men speak well of you" (6:26a). All applause and no criticism isn't necessarily a good thing. If we're speaking God's truth, we're bound to offend some people. Remembering that criticism is inevitable keeps our feet on the ground and our souls attuned to the Spirit.

How He Responded to a Crowd

From the challenge of personal praise, Jesus next contends with the complexities of growing popularity. Luke is subtle but to the point: "And as the crowds were increasing" (11:29a).

Jesus had fame and success from a numbers point of view; in today's terms, His was a million-dollar ministry. This kind of celebrity fervor has the potential of whisking any leader away in the swift currents of at least three temptations:

- to tell people what they want to hear so they'll keep coming back,
- to soften the blows of truth to avoid offending people,
- to tantalize with slick entertainment, competing with the world.

Yet Jesus stood firm, like a rock in the center of a rushing river. First, *He told the truth*.

> "This generation is a wicked generation; it seeks for a sign, and yet no sign shall be given to it but the sign of Jonah. For just as Jonah became a sign to the Ninevites, so shall the Son of Man be to this generation." (vv. 29b–30)

"Enough with the signs!" Jesus said. "You don't want a Savior—you want a stuntman." The people's demand for signs was only a smoke screen for their lack of faith. So He countered, "Let Jonah be your sign."

When Jonah preached repentance in Nineveh, he bore the

marks of three days in the belly of a fish. He was a walking miracle! One look at him, and the people trembled. Jesus, too, was a walking miracle: God in the flesh. What more did the people need in order to believe?

Furthermore, as God rescued Jonah from the fish, so He would deliver Jesus (after three days) from the grave. Want a sign? Just wait until the Resurrection.

The second way Jesus responded to the increasing crowds was this: *He gave them substance*—a historical perspective of the big picture, first with Jonah and next with the Queen of Sheba.

> "The Queen of the South shall rise up with the men of this generation at the judgment and condemn them, because she came from the ends of the earth to hear the wisdom of Solomon; and behold, something greater than Solomon is here. The men of Nineveh shall stand up with this generation at the judgment and condemn it, because they repented at the preaching of Jonah; and behold, something greater than Jonah is here." (vv. 31–32)

By referring to the Ninevites and the Queen of Sheba (see 1 Kings 10:1–13), Jesus made His Jewish audience think. Here were two examples, from Israel's own history, of Gentiles—*Gentiles*—responding with soft hearts to the God of the Jews. Yet the Jews, God's chosen people, had hardened their hearts toward God's Son. How convicting!

In these verses, notice that the focus is on the person of Christ. His wisdom is greater than Solomon's; His preaching is greater than Jonah's. Christ's example drives us to ask ourselves, What is the focal point of our message? Is the light of our ministry shining on Christ?

Third, *Jesus placed responsibility on the hearers*. Jesus strove to present a clear, meaningful message, but He knew that the response was up to those who listened.

> "No one, after lighting a lamp, puts it away in a cellar, nor under a peck-measure, but on the lampstand, in order that those who enter may see the light. The lamp of your body is your eye; when your eye is clear, your whole body also is full of light; but when it is bad, your body also is full of darkness." (Luke 11:33–34)

The leader's job is to light the lamp; the hearer's responsibility is to receive the light. However, if unbelief has closed a person's eyes to the truth, his or her heart will remain dark. People must want to see before Christ can enlighten them.

Fourth and finally, *He warned against self-enlightenment.*

> "Then watch out that the light in *you* may not be darkness. If therefore your whole body is full of light, with no dark part in it, it shall be wholly illumined, as when the lamp illumines you with its rays." (vv. 35–36, emphasis added)

One modern philosophy that disguises darkness as inner light is the New Age movement. Its teachers say that *we* are the light, *we* are god, *we* are what we've been looking for. But in the end, this new "god" betrays us with its emptiness. How much wiser it is to open ourselves in faith to the only true source of light Himself, Jesus Christ.

Some Perils and Principles of "Success"

Jesus' candid and uncompromising approach with His growing following reflects three implications for leaders today. Let's look at them in terms of perils to avoid and principles to follow.

The first peril is personal: *Beware of image building.* We know we're teetering near the edge of this pitfall when we forget who's really in charge—Christ. We start emphasizing doing instead of being. We become obsessed with programs over people. We highlight our adequacies rather than admit our inadequacies. Our attitude rings out *pride, pride, pride.* The corresponding principle? *Keep focusing on reality.* Image building hinders us from concentrating on what's important—the essentials of our calling, our original vision for ministry.

The second peril is organizational: *Beware of becoming a slick business.* Ministries stuck in this hazard live by three words—*competition, competition, competition.* Whatever another ministry does, do it better. Copy the world's methods to accomplish spiritual objectives. The numbers may rise, but the level of spiritual maturity does not. The counteracting principle: *Keep studying Christ.* Duplicate His style, and you'll keep your ministry personal and effective.

The third peril is traditional: *Beware of ignoring the true condition of your heart.* In this snare, we go through the religious motions;

we do whatever it takes to keep smiling and keep the show on the road. Truth is for somebody else. We're fine, no need to change. We exude *indifference, indifference, indifference*. What's the answer? *Keep receiving the light God offers*. Where there's light, there's hope. And where there's hope, there's strength to handle the challenges of leadership.

Living Insights STUDY ONE

You don't have to be a pastor to wear the hat of a spiritual leader. If you've ever given someone spiritual counsel, if you've ever led your family in devotions, if you've ever prayed with someone in pain, if you've ever sat on a committee at church or taught a Sunday school class—you're a spiritual leader.

What leadership role or roles do you fill right now?

Have you started sliding into any of the perilous pitfalls mentioned in the lesson? Evaluate yourself with the following questions.

- Am I image building? If so, how?

- Do my efforts reflect a slick business approach rather than personal, genuine ministry? In what ways?

- Have I been ignoring my heart? What have been the consequences?

Now look at the principles that can help you climb out of the hazard.

- If you've been image building, think back to your original vision for ministry. How can you return to that simpler, purer call?

- If your ministry has turned into a slick business, describe how you intend to make your ministry more personal, more like Christ's.

- If you have been neglecting the condition of your heart, what needs to happen in your life to allow time to receive the restorative light of God's Word?

Leadership may be hazardous, but anything worthwhile has its risks. Don't shy away from your role. With Christ's help, you can avoid the pitfalls and become a leader who is humble and confident, just like Him.

Living Insights STUDY TWO

Flood waters don't have to knock a house down to destroy it—all they have to do is soften the foundation. In time, the building will fall apart under its own weight. That's how, essentially, the waters of success wrecked Jim Bakker's PTL ministry several years ago.

In a revealing interview with *Christianity Today*, Bakker's second in command, Richard Dortch, pointed to success' eroding effects on the spiritual foundation of PTL.

> Sometimes I think the church doesn't know anything about true success. It's all tied to how many stations we have on our network, or how big our building is. It's so easy to lose control, to compromise without recognizing it. At PTL, there was no time taken for prayer or for family, because the show had to go on. We were so caught up in God's work that we forgot about God.[2]

Take a moment to inspect your house. Have you gotten so caught up in God's work that you've forgotten about God? How firm is your foundation?

____

____

____

Don't wait for a tragedy before you start shoring up your spiritual base. How can you begin now to build your foundation so the waters of success cannot damage it?

____

____

____

____

____

2. Richard Dortch, as quoted in "'I Made Mistakes,'" *Christianity Today*, March 18, 1988, p. 47.

Chapter 5

CLEAN . . . FROM THE INSIDE OUT

Luke 11:37–41

Remember your first car? It may not have been a luxury cruiser fresh off the assembly line, but in your eyes it was a peach. It had personality. The horn went *mee-deep* instead of the usual *honk-honk*. The passenger door only opened when you hit the right spot on the side panel. And the engine panted like a puppy waiting for a dog biscuit.

You loved that car. That's why you worried whenever you heard a strange yelp coming from under the hood. Clatter-clatter-clang-sssssssscreech. Oh boy . . . what to do?

Take it to the car wash! That's what it needs. A good lather and polish will make it run like new.

Well . . . that didn't help. Buy it a new radio! Some tunes will make it feel better, or at least drown out the rattle.

Nope. How about this—drive it harder! Rev up the engine as fast as it will go, and maybe it will fix itself?

Don't think so. There's only one way to fix an engine: open the hood, reach deep into the greasy snarl of wires and metal, and repair the damaged parts. Internal problems require internal solutions.

It's a simple principle but one we sometimes ignore when it comes to fixing our hearts. We feel guilty, so we apply some shine to our appearance by giving more money to charities. Depressing thoughts clatter in our heads, so we buy new toys or new clothes to make us feel better—for the moment. Anger bangs and rattles inside, so we drive ourselves harder, hoping the noise will go away.

But it doesn't go away. Damaged hearts require spiritual repairs. Simply polishing the exterior of our lives with religion isn't enough.

Two Distinctions We Must Always Remember

What Christ offers us spiritually differs distinctly from what religion offers in at least two ways.

Ceremonial Symbolism versus Actual Reality

For centuries within the church, ceremonial symbols have

represented the actual realities of our life in Christ. A problem occurs, however, when the symbols themselves overshadow what they represent.

In communion, for example, we eat the bread and drink from the cup to express our trust in the Savior, who redeemed us on the cross. However, the bread and the juice in themselves provide no spiritual nourishment apart from faith in Christ. They are only symbols; the reality is Christ's redemption.

If you were traveling and someone asked to see your family, you'd probably show a snapshot, wouldn't you? Yet that's only a glossy slip of paper, not your family. In the same way, the Lord's Table is only a picture of what Christ did for us, not our actual salvation.

Christ wants us to focus on what the symbols really mean, while religion would only have us dutifully and correctly observe the symbolic ceremonies.

External Washing versus Internal Cleansing

Similarly, religion often promotes external washing, while Christ insists on internal cleansing. It's one thing to polish up our appearances by scrupulously conforming to a strict set of dos and don'ts; it's another thing entirely to open our hearts to God's Spirit and invite Him to change us from within. Inner cleansing means saying, "Lord, here is all the dirt in my life—my pride, my greed, my lust. Forgive me. Heal me. Make me new."

Pharisees, unfortunately, modern and ancient, never understand this distinction. They scrub and scour their lives with the Brillo pad of religious duty until not one speck of grime remains. On the outside, they sparkle. On the inside, they are full of filth.

Jesus confronted the Pharisees of His day on both issues. They continually substituted ceremonial symbols for spiritual reality and external washing for internal cleansing. In Jesus' mind, it was time to peel away their varnished exterior and expose the rottenness underneath.

How Jesus Addressed Both Issues

The opportune moment came when a Pharisee invited Jesus into his home.

An Invitation to Lunch

> Now when He had spoken, a Pharisee asked Him

> to have lunch with him; and He went in, and reclined at the table.[1] (Luke 11:37)

Why would a Pharisee invite Jesus over for a bite to eat? To enjoy the pleasure of His company? To share the riches of Scripture together? To talk privately about some concerns in his walk with God? Most likely not. If we look ahead to verse 45, we see that a group of specialists in the Law were there also. So, from the moment Jesus stepped into the house, the hungry eyes of the religious leaders were sizing up everything He said and did. He had been invited for lunch—but as the main course.

Obviously, Jesus knew this. And He knew exactly how to give the Pharisees a memorable case of indigestion. In fact, He has already done it when He reclined at the table. Did you notice?

An Opportunity to Instruct

The Pharisee certainly noticed.

> And when the Pharisee saw it, he was surprised that He had not first ceremonially washed before the meal. (v. 38)

While everyone else was lining up by the basin, Jesus had squeezed past and seated Himself. That seems a bit rude. Why didn't Jesus wash His hands before He ate?

Drawing on Jewish history, commentator William Barclay sets a place for us at this unusual banquet and helps us understand the issue here.

> This hand-washing was *not* in the interests of hygienic purity; it was *ceremonial cleanness* which was at stake. Before every meal, and between each of the courses, the hands had to be washed, and they had to be washed in a certain way. The hands, to begin with, had to be free of any coating of sand or mortar or gravel or any such substance. The water for washing had to be kept in special large stone jars, so that it itself was clean in the ceremonial sense and so that it might be certain that it had been used for no other purpose, and that nothing had fallen

1. The dining tables were low to the ground, like the ones we might see in Japan today. People reclined on pillows, leaning on the left elbow and eating with the right hand.

> into it or had been mixed with it. First, the hands were held with finger tips *pointing upwards;* water was poured over them and had to run at least down to the wrist; the minimum amount of water was one quarter of a log, which is equal to one and a half egg shells full of water. While the hands were still wet each hand had to be cleansed with the fist of the other. . . . At this stage the hands were wet with water; but that water was now unclean because it had touched unclean hands. So, next, the hands had to be held with finger tips pointing downwards and water had to be poured over them in such a way that it began at the wrists and ran off at the finger tips. After all that had been done the hands were clean.
>
> To fail to do this was in Jewish eyes, not to be guilty of bad manners, not to be dirty in the health sense, but to be unclean in the sight of God.[2]

The Pharisees truly believed they could rinse away the day's defilement by ceremonially washing their hands. Where did they get such a notion? Mark tells us these laws came from "the traditions of the elders" (Mark 7:3). Centuries earlier, pious men took it upon themselves to "help" others by further defining the Law's grand principles. Over time, these rules were etched in stone alongside God's commandments, with thousands more, until the fine print marred the spirit of the Law. By rejecting this single man-made ceremony, Jesus smashed their clay tablets right in front of their eyes. It was the only way He could teach them that sin is an inner problem requiring an inner solution. It's a matter of the heart, not the hands.

> But the Lord said to him, "Now you Pharisees clean the outside of the cup and of the platter; but inside of you, you are full of robbery and wickedness. You foolish ones, did not He who made the outside make the inside also?" (Luke 11:39–40)

Clean dishes and clean hands do not equal clean lives. We can't hide a dirty heart under a layer of ceremonies and religion; God

2. William Barclay, *The Gospel of Mark*, rev. ed., The Daily Study Bible Series (Philadelphia, Pa.: Westminster Press, 1975), pp. 164–65.

knows us inside out. And, according to Jesus, cleansing from the inside out is the only way we can be pure.

An Example of True Cleanliness

In contrast to the reams of rules the Pharisees had for achieving cleanness, Jesus had only one instruction:

> "But give that which is within as charity, and then all things are clean for you."[3] (v. 41)

Love, Jesus says, is the sign of a pure heart. Remember His parable of the good Samaritan, who stopped and cared for the wounded man while the sanctimonious priest and Levite skirted by? In the story, as well as in real life, it's easy to tell whose heart is clean by the love shining through the person's life.

When Putting This into Practice

We marvel at the Pharisees trying to atone for their sins by washing their hands. Yet are we much different? Wanting to look holy, we pour water over our lives as we perform our Sunday morning routines. We try our best to hold our hands properly. To say the right words. To wear the right clothes. To do the right things. Us, lose our tempers? Lust? Slander? Envy? Never! How could you say such a thing when our Christian smiles are so bright?

Christ, however, isn't fooled by our appearance. He wants us to stop pretending and start caring about having a clean heart. Two principles from His lesson can help us avoid the religious hypocrisy of the Pharisees.

First, *never try to cover wrong within by cleaning up the externals of your life*. Just as we can't fix an engine by washing the car, so we can't fix our sinfulness by sprinkling some religion over the surface of our lives. To feel truly clean, we must invite Christ into our inner chambers.

Second, *always pay attention to the inside of your life*. Living in a cosmetic world, we have at our fingertips everything we could ever need to look better than we are. But God sees behind our masks. The writer to the Hebrews says,

> And there is no creature hidden from His sight, but

3. Jesus' pronouncement that "all things are clean for you" foreshadows Peter's vision of the sheet in Acts 10:9–16, in which the Lord declares all animals clean.

all things are open and laid bare to the eyes of Him with whom we have to do. (Heb. 4:13)

Don't be afraid to lay your life bare before God. He knows all about the dirt you've been sweeping under the rug, and He won't be shocked. He wants to give you the wonderful feeling of being clean . . . from the inside out.

Living Insights STUDY ONE

Have you forgotten what it's like to feel clean? With a poet's flare, Walter Wangerin, Jr., conjures up childhood memories of his mother's spring-cleaning and the wonderful way he felt when it was all through.

> We children would wake in the early morning to a sudden bluster of wind through the house. Mom had thrown open all the windows upstairs and down, front and back, living room and our own bedrooms. The curtains blew in and clapped above us: *Get up! Get up! This is the Day of Atonement!*
>
> We stumbled up to find that Mom had propped the front door open and the back door and the basement. We sailed through windy hallways.
>
> Mother herself never paused the day long. She bound her hair in a bandanna blue with white polka dots; she wore weird pants called "pedal-pushers" and rubber gloves and a man's shirt and red canvas shoes with rubber soles: silent, swift, and terrible was she!
>
> Rugs came up and were hung on lines outside for beatings. Her right arm got victories that day. Rugs coughed dark clouds into the yard, and then the hardwood floors were waxed with such power to such a marvelous shine that we, in sock-feet, slipped the surface, surfing. Clean is a feeling beneath your feet.
>
> The curtains came down to be washed. The naked windows squeaked under Windex and newspaper. Mom's dust rag made the Venetian blinds clatter and complain. Bright light flooded the rooms. . . .
>
> Out with the old, then! Out with the bad. My mother was a purging white storm, focused and

furious. Out with the sullen, germ-infested air, colds and flus and fevers. In with the spring! In with lily breezes!

In buckets Mom made elixirs of Spic and Span. She shook Old Dutch Cleanser on sinks as if it were a stick to scold. Throughout the house went ammonia smells, pine smells, soap smells, sudsy smells that canceled sweats and miasmas.

Winter clothes were washed and packed away. Summer wear appeared. Our very bodies lightened, brightened, beamed in newness and health. . . .

By evening we ourselves were bathed, the dust of the day removed, leaving a creamy me.

And this, finally, was the finest comfort of the sacred day: that when I went to bed that night, I slipped my silver self between clean sheets. Sheets sun-dried and wind-softened and smoother to my tender flesh than four white petals of the dogwood tree.[4]

Spiritually, Christ longs to wrap us in that same feeling of clean. But we must invite Him into our heart's home—to bring His buckets and brushes and brooms, to purge the sin-infested air and fill us with "newness and health." To slip us between the sun-dried, wind-softened sheets of His righteousness.

> If we confess our sins, He is faithful and righteous to forgive us our sins and to cleanse us from all unrighteousness. (1 John 1:9)

Won't you confess those sins you have been harboring in your soul's winter? Only Jesus can fill your heart with spring.

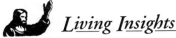

Living Insights STUDY TWO

A great tree once arched its branches over a lush lawn beside a library. Over the years, children ate picnics beneath its arms. They hoisted each other up to play on its broad shoulders. Students lounged in its shade. Couples snuggled under its canopy and carved their dreams on its trunk.

4. Walter Wangerin, Jr., *Little Lamb, Who Made Thee? A Book about Children and Parents* (Grand Rapids, Mich.: Zondervan Publishing House, 1993), pp. 28–29.

The old tree had seen a generation come and go. As long as the sun kept rising, it seemed the tree would stand. Who would have guessed it was dying inside?

Beneath its thick bark, a disease was rotting away the inner rings of its life. Still, every year, it put out its leaves. It held its limbs high. It served its purpose. Until one day, the weight of the huge branches split the trunk and it toppled to the ground. Only then did everyone know the truth.

We can be like that tree. Surrounded by people. Watching. Protecting. Giving. But never revealing our inner struggles. The Pharisees tried to cover themselves with the thick bark of religion. Are you hiding as well? If so, what is your bark made of?

____

____

____

____

God wants to peel away our pretenses to heal the disease that's rotting us inside. Jesus said, "Did not He who made the outside make the inside also?" (Luke 11:40). He knows the truth about you. Does anyone else know? To whom can you open up?

____

You may have toyed with the idea before, but now it's time to do it. Tell someone about your bitter feelings, your disappointments, your struggles. No one can keep secrets like those hidden forever. Won't you start your healing process today?

Chapter 6

OLD PHARISEES NEVER DIE

Luke 11:42–54

Once in a while, Jesus uncaged His anger and let it roar. His eyes flashed. His voice boomed. His holy wrath lashed out at the wickedness around Him. Artists rarely portray this furious side of Christ, preferring to paint Him blessing the multitudes, welcoming the children, cradling a lamb. But pouncing on people? *Not* the Jesus we know.

But we should know that side of Him. The things that anger our Lord reveal a lot about His character, His justice, His holiness. They also reveal what is truly wrong in this world and worth getting upset about.

What unleashed the lion in Christ most often? Religious hypocrisy. And the people who embodied that most notably were the ones whose name has become synonymous with the word *hypocrisy*—the Pharisees.

Understanding How Pharisees Think and Act

Whether plaguing Jesus in the first century or assaulting us today, Pharisees suffocate grace and joy with fiery zeal. Why? What makes them burn so? Let's carefully pick our way through their smoldering thoughts and explore the inner workings of Pharisees.

First, they think only in terms of rules and regulations, so they act legalistically. Like computers, their brains spit out page after page of preprogrammed moral calculations: Do this, but don't do that; follow me and you're in, but disagree and you're out. Their rules have no elasticity. As Max Lucado writes, "Legalism has no pity on people. Legalism: makes my opinion your burden . . . makes my opinion your boundary . . . makes my opinion your obligation."[1] Pharisees leave no room for discovery or disagreement or dialogue.

Second, they think only of themselves, so they act selfishly. The fire in their souls does not burn for love of people. Their passion is for polishing their own image—upright, high-minded, above the

1. Max Lucado, *UpWords* newsletter, May 1993, p. 2.

crowd. With a "righteousness" beyond anyone's reach, they are beyond reaching out to others. They have no humility. Underneath their gleaming religious exterior, their hearts are coated with the soot of pride.

Third, they think only in black and white, so they act judgmentally. Every action is categorized as either right or wrong. And who decides which is which? They do. They have no leniency, give no second chances. Either conform or be judged.

Are we being unfair to Pharisees? Is our critique too harsh? Well, look at the harsh light Jesus cast on them in Matthew 6.

> "Beware of practicing your righteousness before men to be noticed by them; otherwise you have no reward with your Father who is in heaven.
>
> "When therefore you give alms, do not sound a trumpet before you, as the hypocrites do in the synagogues and in the streets, that they may be honored by men. Truly I say to you, they have their reward in full. . . .
>
> "And when you pray, you are not to be as the hypocrites; for they love to stand and pray in the synagogues and on the street corners, in order to be seen by men. Truly I say to you, they have their reward in full. . . .
>
> "And whenever you fast, do not put on a gloomy face as the hypocrites do, for they neglect their appearance in order to be seen fasting by men. Truly I say to you, they have their reward in full." (vv. 1–2, 5, 16)

"Hypocrites!" Jesus shouted. He boiled with rage at these snakes in white robes slithering around Palestine. God had written His commandments to bring people to Himself, but the Pharisees were poisoning His Law, using it instead for self-promotion. They trumpeted their alms-giving, prayed to gain an audience, fasted for show. "Where is God in all this?" Jesus wanted to know.

Wherever people hide behind masks of spirituality, wherever leaders glorify themselves instead of God, we'll find the poison of Pharisaism. Because old Pharisees never die; they live on in every generation. That is why Jesus fought against them with all His might. And that is why we should listen to Him with all our hearts.

Proclaiming Condemnation against Pharisaism

Having exposed the Pharisees' hypocrisy in their ceremonial hand-washing, Jesus now outright condemns them in six "woes." Three He fires at Pharisees in general, and three more He aims at lawyers—the experts of religious law and cohorts of the Pharisees.

Woe #1: For Observing the Tiniest Tithe yet Disregarding the Greatest Virtues

> "But woe to you Pharisees! For you pay tithe of mint and rue and every kind of garden herb, and yet disregard justice and the love of God; but these are the things you should have done without neglecting the others." (Luke 11:42)

The Pharisees took to an extreme the Law's requirement to tithe a portion "of the land, of the seed of the land or of the fruit of the tree" (Lev. 27:30). These hypocrites meticulously weighed each sprinkling of herbs from their gardens, but they sloughed off the larger principles of the Law: justice toward others and love toward God.

In Matthew, Jesus shouts at them, "You blind guides, who strain out a gnat and swallow a camel!" (23:24). They strained out every tiny infraction from their cup of duty to God, but then they swallowed a camel-sized offense against a neighbor. According to Jesus, loving God and loving people go hand in hand (see Mark 12:30–31). Tithing to God and fairness to people is not an either/or proposition. According to Him, it's both/and.

Woe #2: For Craving Religious Limelight and Public Applause

> "Woe to you Pharisees! For you love the front seats in the synagogues, and the respectful greetings in the market places." (Luke 11:43)

Unlike the first row in a church, which is often reluctantly filled by latecomers, the front seats in the synagogue faced the congregation and were reserved for the most distinguished guests. The Pharisees clamored for these seats. They relished the pomp of being escorted to the front. They loved to sit there like kings, surveying their court and basking in the admiration of their subjects.

They also loved "respectful greetings," public announcements in the streets. These splashes of verbal recognition would send ripples of whispers through a crowded marketplace. *Pharisee Benjamin is here! Surely, you've heard about him. There he is!*

The lesson for us is, Beware of seeking personal fame in the name of religion. Jesus condemns that sort of grandstanding. He values character, not religious titles and seats of honor.

Woe #3: For Deceiving Others into Becoming Defiled

> "Woe to you! For you are like concealed tombs, and the people who walk over them are unaware of it." (v. 44)

A little background information from commentator William Hendriksen helps us decipher this verse:

> According to a Jewish custom, just before the arrival of vast caravans of people traveling to Jerusalem to attend the Passover, graves were whitewashed. The reason this was done was that they might be clearly visible, so that no one would ceremonially defile himself by walking over a grave.[2]

Jesus was saying, "Somebody should have whitewashed you Pharisees!" Not only were they as defiled as a tomb full of rotting bones, they were contaminating unsuspecting passersby who followed in their steps.

Jesus couldn't have stabbed them with a more painful insult. In their eyes, the decay of death covered sinners, not them. Their lives shone with moral purity. Yet from Jesus' point of view, a humble sinner was more worthy than a sanctimonious Pharisee (see 18:9–14).

By now, the Pharisee hosting Jesus must have been seething with humiliation and rage. Perhaps realizing he was outmanned, he said nothing in return. Instead, the lawyers stepped forward, only to receive a verbal swipe themselves.

Woe #4: For Adding to Others' Guilt without Assuming Any Themselves

> And one of the lawyers said to Him in reply, "Teacher, when You say this, You insult us too." But He said, "Woe to you lawyers as well! For you weigh

2. William Hendriksen, *Exposition of the Gospel according to Luke*, New Testament Commentary Series (Grand Rapids, Mich.: Baker Book House, 1978), p. 640.

> men down with burdens hard to bear, while you yourselves will not even touch the burdens with one of your fingers." (11:45–46)

How could these experts in the Law get away with not keeping their own laws? "Because they were experts in evasion," writes William Barclay.[3] Here is just one of their many legal tricks.

> One of the forbidden works on the Sabbath was the tying of knots, sailors' or camel drivers' knots and knots in ropes. But a woman might tie the knot in her girdle. Therefore, if a bucket of water had to be raised from a well a rope could not be knotted to it, but a woman's girdle could, and it could be raised with that![4]

How ridiculous! Raise a water bucket with rope—sin. With a girdle—not sin. What kind of God would stipulate a silly law like that? Yet these scribes—as they were also called—spent their lives chiseling out these convoluted rules and piling them like stones on people's backs.

Woe #5: For Faking Obedience While Looking Pious

> "Woe to you! For you build the tombs of the prophets, and it was your fathers who killed them." (v. 47)

Trying to impress people, the scribes were constructing or remodeling monuments to the dead prophets. Yet, ironically, none of them were building their lives on what the prophets had taught. Where were their acts of justice or kindness? How were they walking humbly with God (see Mic. 6:8)?

Jesus declared that their only true link to the prophets was through their fathers—who killed the prophets in the first place. By finishing the tombs, they were simply completing the job their forebears started.

> "Consequently, you are witnesses and approve the deeds of your fathers; because it was they who killed them, and you build their tombs. For this reason also

3. William Barclay, *The Gospel of Luke*, rev. ed., The Daily Bible Study Series (Philadelphia, Pa.: Westminster Press, 1975), p. 158.

4. Barclay, *The Gospel of Luke*, p. 158.

> the wisdom of God said, 'I will send to them prophets and apostles, and some of them they will kill and some they will persecute, in order that the blood of all the prophets, shed since the foundation of the world, may be charged against this generation, from the blood of Abel to the blood of Zechariah, who perished between the altar and the house of God; yes, I tell you, it shall be charged against this generation.'" (Luke 11:48–51)

Abel's murder is recorded in Genesis (4:8), Zechariah's in 2 Chronicles (24:20–21)—the first and last books of the Hebrew Bible. Jesus was saying that from Abel to Zechariah, from beginning to end, the blood of the martyrs was on their hands. Why? Because their hearts harbored the same hateful spirit as the murderers who came before them.

Woe #6: For Substituting Works for Faith

> "Woe to you lawyers! For you have taken away the key of knowledge; you did not enter in yourselves, and those who were entering in you hindered." (Luke 11:52)

No one knew the Bible better than these religious scholars. Their knowledge could have unlocked the door to the Messiah and God's kingdom, but they concealed their key. They twisted Scripture into "a book of riddles," writes Barclay.

> In their mistaken ingenuity they refused to see its plain meaning themselves, and they would not let anyone else see it either. The scriptures had become the perquisite of the expert and a dark mystery to the common man.[5]

Each of Jesus' six woes stripped away layer after layer of hypocrisy until the lawyers' and the Pharisees' true faces could be seen. Were His charges against them justified? Beneath their masks, were they really as depraved as He made them out to be? Luke answers us in verses 53–54.

> And when He left there, the scribes and the

5. Barclay, *The Gospel of Luke*, p. 159.

> Pharisees began to be very hostile and to question Him closely on many subjects, plotting against Him, to catch Him in something He might say.

This word *very*, in Greek *deinōs*, means "terribly, vehemently, violently."[6] It is the root for the prefix in *dinosaur*, which literally means "terrifying lizard."[7] No more would the Pharisees feign cordiality toward Jesus. He had stripped them of their silken piety and exposed their scaly, reptilian souls. So they would retaliate. In every city they would stalk Him, hungrily striking at His words to distort and use them against Him. Only His death would satisfy their taste for blood.

Changing a Pharisaic Mind-set: What Will It Take?

Jesus fought the Pharisees all the way to the Cross. Today legalists and hypocrites still do the worst damage to the cause of Christ. Can modern Pharisees be helped? What does it take?

First, *it takes an inescapable event that gets their attention*. Tragedies like a failed marriage, a lost reputation, an emotional breakdown often strip away masks and open eyes to the truth.

Second, *it takes an unconditional admission*. "I'm guilty. I'm proud. I'm a hypocrite. I tend to demand my way. Have mercy on me, Lord, I repent." These are the confessions of a person with a soft heart and a receptive spirit—which the Lord always honors.

Third, *it takes an unqualified willingness to change*. Prejudicial ways of thinking, intolerant attitudes, judgmental habits—all must be transformed. It's a painful process at first, but one that leads to freedom. Freedom from endless lists of man-made rules. Freedom from having to live up to everyone else's expectations. Freedom from fear.

Freedom to love God and others the way Christ intended.

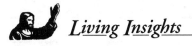

Living Insights — STUDY ONE

If Jesus were to physically stand before His church today, He'd undoubtedly warn us: "Beware of shaping your spirituality for the

6. Hendriksen, *The Gospel according to Luke*, p. 647.

7. *Merriam-Webster's Collegiate Dictionary*, 10th ed., see "dinosaur."

purpose of impressing other people." He would want us to root out Pharisaism both corporately and privately.

What is He saying to you? Do any of His "woes" to the Pharisees prick at your heart? Pray that you might hear His message for you, and ask for His Spirit's guidance as you consider the following questions related to the Pharisees' faults that were uncovered in our chapter.

- **Observing the Tiniest Tithe yet Disregarding the Greatest Virtues**

It's easy to focus on "gnat" issues, like worship, clothing, and hairstyles, while leaving the "camels" unattended—kindness, justice, forgiveness. What tends to occupy your mind, the tiny issues of Christianity or the important ones?

____

____

If you need to, what will you change?

____

____

____

- **Craving Religious Limelight and Public Applause**

Jesus addresses motives here. Why do you study the Bible? Memorize verses? Attend seminars? Pray? Sing? Serve? Do you seek recognition and admiration? If no one saw your spirituality, would you still be as dedicated to Christ?

____

____

____

- **Deceiving Others into Becoming Defiled**

Is your teaching or counsel anchored in Scripture? Think of a recent situation in which you were giving someone spiritual advice. Were you drawing your principles from God's Word or pulling them

out of your own opinions?

In the next Living Insight, we'll open our hearts to Jesus' three other "woeful" areas.

Living Insights STUDY TWO

Again, pray and wait for the Spirit's direction as you think over the following Pharisaic faults and corresponding questions.

- **Adding to Others' Guilt without Assuming Any Themselves**

It's easy to judge others for the things we do ourselves. We deem the R-rated movie in the theater bad, but we'll watch it on video. We condemn others for smoking, while we overeat. We distance ourselves from dirty language, but we pull up close to gossip. The list goes on and on.

What do you judge others for? Do you practice the same sin in another form?

- **Faking Obedience While Looking Pious**

On Sundays, we dress in our best to show respect for the Lord. Or do we? For many people, Sunday morning is a time to scrub up their facades and try to look holy. "There aren't any problems in this dry-cleaned, clean-cut family."

Are you tempted to put on a show of piety before others? How is it expressed?

- **Substituting Works for Faith**

The lawyers and Pharisees had no room for Christ because they had no room for faith. To them, salvation depended on their works—what they could do for God, not what God could do for them.

Do you see yourself slipping into this Pharisaic mind-set? In what ways?

___

___

___

What do Christ's words show you? Do you notice traces of hypocrisy? A judgmental spirit? Pharisaic pride? Confess those tendencies to the Lord. Tell Him that you're willing to change. And you will.

Chapter 7

Marching Orders for True Disciples

Luke 12:1–12

Having dared to speak against the Pharisees, Jesus would now be hounded by them until He was either powerless or dead. Everywhere He turned, the religious leaders, like secret police, would be lurking in the shadows, watching . . . listening . . . plotting. Luke's twelfth chapter opens with a reference to this hostile setting, "Under these circumstances"—under these intimidating, perilous circumstances.

Jesus knew His time was short. Every hour, every minute that passed was like the beating of a drum, pounding out His death march to the Cross. Commentators call this section of His life the Later Judean Ministry—the last six months before Calvary.

Wherever He went, His presence charged the air with expectancy. The crowds grew larger and more frenzied. Luke describes their almost riotous response to Him:

> So many thousands of the multitude had gathered together that they were stepping on one another. (v. 1a)

Public adoration is a fickle wind, though. Some of these same people would soon be stepping over themselves shouting for His crucifixion before Pilate. These were turbulent times—times that made Jesus' instructions to the disciples all the more vital.

The Instructions: Several Commands worth Obeying

Although the Pharisees are bearing down on Him and the crowds are clamoring for His attention, Jesus focuses His energies on His men. Their survival depends on their battle preparation, so Jesus issues four commands to His troops—marching orders that will guide them to victory.

Beware of Living the Life of a Hypocrite

Jesus gives His first command in verse 1b:

> "Beware of the leaven of the Pharisees, which is hypocrisy."

Leaven, or yeast, permeates dough and makes it rise. It doesn't affect just one part—it alters the whole batch (see 1 Cor. 5:6). Hypocrisy, Jesus warns, acts the same way. It permeates a person's heart and puffs it up with pride. It disfigures a person's entire life and ministry.

What makes hypocrisy so potent a sin? *Deception*. Hypocrisy is a costume ball where we deny we're wearing costumes. It's piety put on to convince people that we're better than we really are. The word originated with the Greek stage, in which actors—*hupokritēs*—wore masks when they played their roles. The Pharisees were also accomplished performers. They masked their pride and greed behind a face of holiness that fooled many people into thinking they were righteous—including themselves. But they couldn't fool God. And neither can we. As Jesus says,

> "There is nothing covered up that will not be revealed, and hidden that will not be known. Accordingly, whatever you have said in the dark shall be heard in the light, and what you have whispered in the inner rooms shall be proclaimed upon the housetops." (Luke 12:2–3)

How senseless to hide, yet how often we try! The sensual thoughts, the jealousies, the manipulations, the anger—because we're human we will feel them, but because we're sinful we will foster them in the inner rooms of our hearts. Yet would we ever admit their existence? Or when someone else confesses them, do we act shocked and give the impression that we've never sunk *that* low? How foolish!

"Where can I go from Thy Spirit?" David asked God. "Or where can I flee from Thy presence?" Not to the highest heaven, the deepest underworld, the earliest dawn, or the loneliest sea. "Even the darkness is not dark to Thee . . . Darkness and light are alike to Thee" (Ps. 139:7–12). The Lord sees all: "There is no creature hidden from His sight, but all things are open and laid bare" (Heb. 4:13). And one day all those things we vainly try to keep secret, from Him and from ourselves, will be judged through Jesus (Rom. 2:16).

So, contrary to the infectious leaven of the Pharisees, Jesus' countermand is this: Be authentic. Be the same in the light as in the dark. Don't be a phony.

Do Not Fear Physical Harm or Death, but Fear the Lord

Hypocrites don't often welcome their pretenses being stripped away, as the Pharisees reveal. Rather than giving up their show and seeking a truly full life, they have turned with fury on the One who dared expose their emptiness. In light of their murderous intent, Jesus provides a second strategy: Fear God instead of people.

Jesus knows the conflicts in store for His disciples: imprisonments, beatings, even martyrdom. To put steel in their backbones and hope in their hearts, He gives them, and us, three reasons not to be afraid.

First, people may harm the body, but they can't harm the soul. Only God has authority over that which is eternal.

> "And I say to you, My friends, do not be afraid of those who kill the body, and after that have no more that they can do. But I will warn you whom to fear: fear the One who after He has killed has authority to cast into hell; yes, I tell you, fear Him!" (Luke 12:4–5)

That's enough to terrorize us. Is this Jesus' purpose? No, but He does intend to place fear where it properly belongs. Too often our earthly anxieties wither our view of God and magnify themselves. So Jesus smashes these oversized images and brings our eyes back to the only real God, the only One worthy to be feared.

But fear is not where Jesus would leave us. His next words quiet our hearts by reminding us of God's gentle, attentive care.

> "Are not five sparrows sold for two cents? And yet not one of them is forgotten before God." (v. 6)

If God will not forget something so small, something we deem worth less than a penny apiece, then surely He'll remember us. When His enemies strike at us, Jesus reassures that we won't slip God's mind. So our second reason for not being afraid is that no matter what happens, God will not forget us.

And third, we can take courage in the fact that we are valuable to Him.

> "Indeed, the very hairs of your head are all numbered. Do not fear; you are of more value than many sparrows." (v. 7)

From "Fear Him!" in verse 5 to "Do not fear" in verse 7, Jesus has taken us from somber awe to comforted joy. For no one else knows us as well or loves us as much as God does. And no one—not the most vicious, cunning enemy—is more powerful than this God who values us.

The best way to conquer the fear of people is to fear God. He is the mighty Judge who can touch the soul and give eternal life or eternal death. He is the all-knowing Lover who truly cares for us. And it is His opinion of us that matters most.

Confess the Son of Man Openly

Jesus' third marching order divides the hearts of Pharisees from the hearts of true disciples.

> "And I say to you, everyone who confesses Me before men, the Son of Man shall confess him also before the angels of God; but he who denies Me before men shall be denied before the angels of God. And everyone who will speak a word against the Son of Man, it shall be forgiven him; but he who blasphemes against the Holy Spirit, it shall not be forgiven him." (vv. 8–10)

As Christ's soldiers, we don't stand for a lofty principle; we stand for a Person. We fight under Jesus' flag, defend Jesus' honor, confess Jesus' name. The Enemy's troops, however, deny He is the Son of God . . . so He, in turn, will deny them in heaven.

But as long as there is life, there is a lifeline of hope from Jesus' heart. Even those who speak against Him can turn and find forgiveness. Yet, if they blaspheme against the Holy Spirit, there is no way back (see also Matt. 12:31–32). The Pharisees blasphemed the Holy Spirit when they ascribed to Beelzebul the Spirit's miraculous works through Jesus (see vv. 22–24). According to William Barclay, that action capped a long history of rejecting God and forever closed the door on their chance of salvation.

> By repeatedly refusing God's word, by repeatedly taking our own way, by repeatedly shutting our eyes to God and closing our ears to him, we can come to a stage when we do not recognize him when we see him, when to us evil becomes good and good becomes evil. That is what happened to the scribes and Pharisees. They had so blinded and deafened

> themselves to God that when he came they called him the devil.
>
> Why is that the unforgivable sin? Because in such a state *repentance is impossible*. If a man does not even realize that he is sinning, if goodness no longer makes any appeal to him, he cannot repent. God has not shut him out; by his repeated refusals he has shut himself out.[1]

Do Not Become Anxious about Defending Yourself

Jesus' fourth order addresses the disciples' natural tendency to worry about how they would defend themselves against the bitter and hardened Pharisees.

> "And when they bring you before the synagogues and the rulers and the authorities, do not become anxious about how or what you should speak in your defense, or what you should say; for the Holy Spirit will teach you in that very hour what you ought to say." (Luke 12:11–12)

Notice that Jesus said *when*, not *if*. The disciples were destined to stand trial before hostile religious and civic courts; and we, too, will face inevitable opposition as followers of Christ. Yet Jesus says not to worry. Why not? Scripture gives us three reasons.

First, our own integrity will speak for us (Ps. 26:1). Second, "the battle is the Lord's," as David told Goliath (1 Sam. 17:47). And third, at the critical moment when we need to speak, the Holy Spirit will help us know what to say. Perhaps He'll give us a fresh insight. Or maybe He'll bring to mind a verse we've memorized or a truth we learned long ago. So avoid worry's stranglehold and rest in the Spirit's strength.

The Reactions: Three Responses worth Considering

Today's enemies of Christ launch attacks in all areas of society.

1. William Barclay, *The Gospel of Luke*, rev. ed., The Daily Study Bible Series (Philadelphia, Pa.: Westminster Press, 1975), p. 162. Some people tremble at the thought of an unpardonable sin, supposing they may have unknowingly committed it and have been barred from heaven. But, as Barclay wisely points out, "The one man who can never have committed the unforgivable sin is the man who fears that he has, for once a man has committed it, he is so dead to God that he is conscious of no sin at all" (p. 162).

They bombard us in the media, in the courts, and in the halls of government. Even our children are involved in skirmishes in their schools. How can we follow Christ's marching orders in our battlefields?

First, *if you're a phony, admit it*. Hypocrisy ruins our reputations and makes us trite. It dissolves faith into religious clichés and canned principles. Take a look in the mirror. Is what you see the real you? Face the areas of your life you've been hiding. Don't let hypocrisy squeeze the life out of your faith.

Second, *if you're fearful, redirect it*. Fear of opposition steals our courage and makes us timid. It paints our enemies bigger than they really are. By fearing the Lord, however, we put our world back in proper perspective, with God as all-powerful and in charge.

Third, *if you're worried, stop it*. Worry drains our energy and makes us tired, because prior to the actual battle, we fight the Enemy a hundred times in our minds. Then, when the conflict finally does arise, we're too exhausted and tied up in knots to sense the Spirit's leading. Relax. Untie those knots of anxiety with the settled assurance that the Holy Spirit will be there in your moment of need.

Living Insights STUDY ONE

Three words sum up the qualities Jesus is looking for in His soldiers: authenticity, courage, and confidence. How deeply ingrained are they in your life?

Authenticity

"Whatever you have said in the dark," Jesus said, "shall be heard in the light, and what you have whispered in the inner rooms shall be proclaimed upon the housetops" (Luke 12:3). As you examine your life, do you find any secret whispers that would embarrass you if broadcast from the housetops? Have you recently said or done anything in the dark that would damage your reputation if brought to light? Do you need to take off a spiritual mask?

Write down the one thing you need to change the most to become authentic, and think through how you can begin making this change this week.

Courage

Jesus' regimen to develop courage is to fear the Lord instead of our enemies (Luke 12:4–5). Are you facing an enemy right now? How big does the situation seem to you compared to God? Have you made Him too small?

Remind yourself of God's size and strength by writing down as many truths about His power as you can think of.

Pray that you would know more deeply how intimately God knows you and how immensely He values you. If you like, write down your prayer.

Confidence

Are you feeling under the gun? Have a few enemies of Christ been pressuring you because of your faith? Have you worried about what you should say to them in defense? Describe what you're most anxious about.

What comfort is there in knowing that the Holy Spirit will help you in your hour of need (Luke 12:11–12)?

Living Insights STUDY TWO

Christ calls us to *be* authentic, courageous, and confident, but what does He call us to *do?*

Confess His name.

Think of what the name Jesus Christ means. Jesus—the Savior of the world. Christ—the Anointed One, the Son of God, the Messiah. Everything we do and say either confesses or denies the truth of who He is.

Showing mercy to others reveals the Savior's mercy to us. When we forgive others, people get a taste of His forgiveness. By our holiness, we reflect His purity as the Son of God.

Is your life confessing His name clearly? How accurate is the picture of Christ you're showing your friends and family members?

How about with your words? Have you told anyone lately what Christ means to you? Write down three of Christ's qualities that you'd like to share with someone this week.

Now . . . authentically, courageously, confidently—confess His name.

Chapter 8

TESTIMONY OF A FOOL

Luke 12:13–21

Leo Tolstoy tells the story of a young Russian who inherits his father's small farm. The youth starts dreaming right away of how he can expand his property. Then, one morning, an impressive-looking stranger visits him and makes a tantalizing offer: The youth can have, free of charge, all the property he can walk around in one day—but he must return to the same spot from which he started by sundown, or the deal is canceled. Motioning to the grave of the young man's father, the stranger says: "This is the point to which you must return."

The youth longingly eyes the rich fields in the distance. Without packing provisions or saying good-bye to his family, he throws aside his coat and immediately starts off.

He figures he can cover six square miles in a day. But when he reaches the first turn, he decides to make it nine. Then twelve, and then fifteen square miles. Now he must walk sixty miles before sundown!

By noon he reaches the halfway point. Taking no time for food or water, on and on he goes, his legs aching and his stomach clawing him with hunger. Still several miles from home, he is already fatigued to the point of exhaustion.

Yet his obsession to own the land drives him forward. A few hundred yards from the finish, he sees the sun setting on the horizon. Only minutes remain until sundown. Gathering his strength, he staggers on. Just before the sun sets, he—the new master of fifteen square miles of land—stumbles across the line . . . and collapses on the ground, dead.

The stranger smiles cynically: "I offered him all the land he could cover. Now you see what that is: six feet long by two feet wide; and I thought he would like to have the land close to his father's grave, rather than to have it anywhere else." Having said that, the stranger, whose name is Death, vanishes, saying, "I have kept my pledge."[1]

1. As told by Clarence Edward Macartney, *Macartney's Illustrations* (Nashville, Tenn.: Abingdon-Cokesbury Press, 1946), pp. 26–27.

There's a name for this greedy young man: *fool.* Jesus, too, tells a story about a greedy fool who comes face-to-face with the same stranger. It's a lesson that flashes a warning to all of us about the deadly nature of greed.

An Interruption from Someone in the Crowd

Against the backdrop of a huge, anxious crowd pressing around Him, Jesus has been giving specific marching orders to His disciples. Suddenly, out of the multitude, a certain man elbows his way close enough to blurt out a request.

Request

> "Teacher, tell my brother to divide the family inheritance with me." (Luke 12:13)

More a demand than a request, his statement reveals an inheritance battle that has turned the two brothers into ravenous wolves, tearing at the family spoils. The man is counting on Jesus to get him his money. But Jesus refuses to put His hand between the snarling brothers.

Response

> But He said to him, "Man, who appointed Me a judge or arbiter over you?" (v. 14)

God didn't send His Son to be a judge in a small claims court; He sent Him to save souls. With that higher purpose in mind, Jesus turns the interruption into an instructive moment. The man's brother isn't the enemy—the enemy is the voracious sin that is devouring them both.

> And He said to them, "Beware, and be on your guard against every form of greed." (v. 15a)

Greed—in Greek, *pleonexia*—is "a desire to have more (*pleon*, 'more,' *echō*, 'to have')."[2] It's an insatiable craving that can drive people to self-destruction.

> Picture a shipwrecked sailor on a life raft in the middle of an ocean. His terrible thirst impels him

2. W. E. Vine, Merrill F. Unger, and William White, Jr., *Vine's Expository Dictionary of Biblical Words* (Nashville, Tenn.: Thomas Nelson Publishers, 1985), p. 136.

> to drink the salt water, but it only makes him thirstier. This causes him to drink even more, which makes him thirstier still. He consumes more and more of the salty water . . . until, paradoxically, he becomes dehydrated and dies.[3]

"Beware," Jesus warns. Money and possessions can become toxic substitutes for what will truly satisfy—the pure, living water of Christ. He further cautions,

> "For not even when one has an abundance does his life consist of his possessions." (v. 15b)

Greed tries to convince us of just the opposite—that life does consist of what we own. The more we own, we think, the happier we'll be. Jesus, however, uncovers the futility of this reasoning, correcting our shortsighted perspective with a parable.

A Story Jesus Told

Our priorities get radically adjusted when we look at life from the vantage point of our own grave, as Jesus illustrates.

The Parable of the Rich Fool

> And He told them a parable, saying, "The land of a certain rich man was very productive. And he began reasoning to himself, saying, 'What shall I do, since I have no place to store my crops?' And he said, 'This is what I will do: I will tear down my barns and build larger ones, and there I will store all my grain and my goods. And I will say to my soul, "Soul, you have many goods laid up for many years to come; take your ease, eat, drink and be merry."'" (vv. 16–19)

Lurking in the shadows of this man's heart is avarice, and in this story we catch an ugly glimpse of it. Not when his fields produce a bumper crop—success doesn't necessarily indicate greed. Nor when he decides to build bigger barns—he is simply planning ahead. Greed reveals its treacherous face when the man tells us *why*

3. From the study guide *Living Above the Level of Mediocrity*, rev. and exp., coauthored by Ken Gire, from the Bible-teaching ministry of Charles R. Swindoll (Anaheim, Calif.: Insight for Living, 1994), p. 83.

he's building his barns. He intends to hoard his wealth for himself. He's banking his future on his possessions. A full barn guarantees a full and satisfying life—or so he thinks.

> "But God said to him, 'You fool! This very night your soul is required of you; and now who will own what you have prepared?'" (v. 20)

He can't take his precious grain to the grave. What will happen to it? The wolves will fight over it, just like the two brothers at the beginning of the passage. The man sowed greed in his heart, and when the divine reaper put a sickle to his life, greed was the legacy left for his family.

Commentator William Hendriksen points out this man's two fatal mistakes.[4] First, *he didn't understand himself*. He was an expert at tilling the soil, but he didn't know anything about tending his soul. He saturated his body with temporal comforts, while letting his eternal spirit become parched for lack of nourishment.

Second, *he didn't care about others*. Hendriksen notes that, in the Greek, "the words *I* and *my* occur an even dozen times."[5] Not once does the man look toward heaven and give thanks for God's provision or seek the Lord's guidance with how to spend his surplus. Not once does he look toward other people and think of their needs. All he can see is himself. It is "*my* barns," "*my* grain," "*my* goods" . . . until death strips it all away and leaves the storehouse of his life empty before God.

The Lesson for Everyone

With piercing eyes, Jesus scans the crowd and draws the curtain on His story with a warning:

> "So is the man who lays up treasure for himself, and is not rich toward God." (v. 21)

God called the rich man a fool (v. 20), and so is everyone who substitutes temporal treasures for a rich relationship with God.

The lesson, then, is this: *You're not ready to live until you're ready to die*. Death is a great teacher. Had the man weighed his plans on

4. William Hendriksen, *Exposition of the Gospel according to Luke*, New Testament Commentary Series (Grand Rapids, Mich.: Baker Book House, 1978), p. 663.

5. Hendriksen, *Luke*, p. 663.

the scale of the hereafter, he would have learned what was most valuable in the here and now. Barns packed full of grain will collapse and rot, but a heart overflowing with love for God and kindness toward others will endure forever.

Closing Thoughts on Steering Clear of Greed

Do you battle the temptation to clutch and hoard and guard your earthly treasures? Here are three principles that may help you fend off your real enemy: greed.

First, *when you are blessed with much, give generously*. Even Dickens' money-grubbing Ebenezer Scrooge learned that generosity puts a joy in one's heart that riches can't buy. But does being generous mean that we give everything away? No, Paul advises that we regularly set aside money to give away as the Lord prospers us (see 1 Cor. 16:1–2).

Second, *when you plan for the future, think terminally*. Ask yourself, "What do I want to take with me when I die?" We can't bring our toys. We can't squeeze a briefcase full of money through the gates of heaven. Angels won't accept credit cards, not even the gold ones. What can we take to heaven? The testimonies of the people whose lives we touched with the gospel. The satisfaction of a godly legacy. The spiritual riches we built up in heaven. If we plan our lives around these things, we know we're making sound investments for the future.

Third, *whether you have much or little, hold it loosely*. Don't put your hope in barns filled with grain. Loosen your grip on the things of this world. For with a sudden rush of wind, they can blow out of your hands. Instead, hold on to the Lord, who never lets go of you.

Living Insights — STUDY ONE

If we substitute the word *greed* for *sin* in the following definition by Saint Augustine, we can see a side of greed we may not have noticed before.

> Sin [or greed] comes when we take a perfectly natural desire or longing or ambition and try desperately to fulfill it without God.[6]

6. *The Confessions of Saint Augustine*, as quoted in *Christianity Today*, October 25, 1993, p. 73.

Let's take our longing for security, for example. Jesus promised that we can rest in Him (Matt. 11:28–30). Greed, though, feeds on our fear that He is not sufficient. If we had enough money in the bank, then we would be secure for life. But how much is enough? Greed says, "You can never have enough."

Where is your security?

____

____

____

Our hearts also cry out for happiness. Scripture tells us that the joy of the Lord is our strength (see Neh. 8:10). But we spy a sleek, new sports car sailing down the road, and greed whispers to us, "There goes excitement on wheels. You deserve a piece of that joy."

On what does your happiness depend?

____

____

____

From childhood, we desire a sense of worth. God values each of us (Luke 12:6–7), but the world measures our worth by the yardstick of image. So greed tells us to gather all the clothes, memberships, and status-enhancers we can get our hands on.

What defines your sense of worth?

____

____

____

When we fix our hope on anything but God, we open the door of our hearts to greed. According to 1 Timothy 6:17–19, how can you keep the door bolted?

____

____

____

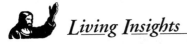

Living Insights STUDY TWO

Ken Gire penetrates the core of Jesus' parable in a moving prayer from his book *Instructive Moments with the Savior*. Read it thoughtfully, letting his words draw out your own desire to become rich toward God.

> Dear Teacher,
>
> Teach me what life is all about.
>
> Help me to learn that it does not consist of possessions, no matter how many, no matter how nice.
>
> Help me to realize that the more things I selfishly accumulate, the more barns I will have to build to store them in. Help me to realize, too, that the storage fee on such things is subtracted from a life that could be rich toward you instead.
>
> Where have I enriched myself at the expense of my soul? Where have I been a fool? Show me, Lord. While there is still time to change.
>
> Teach me that life is more than the things necessary to sustain it. Help me to learn that if life is more than food, surely it is more important than how the dining room looks; if it's more than clothes, certainly it is more important than whether there's enough closet space to hold them.
>
> Keep me from treasuring those things, Lord. I don't want my heart to be stored up in some cupboard or closet the way that rich man's heart was stored up in his barns. I want my heart to be with you, treasuring the things you treasure.
>
> Show me what those things are, Lord.
>
> Sweep my heart clean of every kind of greed. . . .
>
> Help me to realize that just as I brought nothing into this world, so I can take nothing out, and that the only riches I will have in heaven are those which have gone before me, the riches which I have placed in the hands of the poor for your safekeeping. . . .[7]

7. Ken Gire, *Instructive Moments with the Savior* (Grand Rapids, Mich.: Zondervan Publishing House, 1992), pp. 30–31.

Chapter 9

VERTICAL LIVING IN A HORIZONTAL WORLD

Luke 12:22–34

Suppose you could try everything the world has to offer to find happiness. Every year you'd move into a grander home. Designers would continually stock your closets with the latest fashions. You'd own every state-of-the-art "toy" and visit all the world's finest resorts. Would you ever find the end of the rainbow?

Bernard of Clairvaux, a monk from the Middle Ages, shows what you would discover.

> One treasure after another would fail to satisfy, and then the only object of desire left would be the Cause of all. It is our nature's law that makes a man set higher value on the things he has not got than upon those he has, so that he loathes his actual possessions for longing for the things that are not his. And this same law, when all things else in earth and heaven have failed, drives him at last to God, the Lord of all.[1]

Many people squander their lives trying one created thing after another, coming to the Creator only when everything else has failed. Or perhaps never coming. "Theirs is an endless road," added Bernard, "a hopeless maze, who seek for goods before they seek for God."[2] How much wiser we would be to seek God first—which is Jesus' point in our passage.

Why Did Jesus Offer This Instruction?

Jesus' parable of the rich fool taught us that life is not about possessions. Contrary to the popular bumper sticker, those who die with the most toys aren't winners. They're fools for spending all

1. Bernard of Clairvaux, as quoted by John Baillie in A *Diary of Readings* (New York, N.Y.: Macmillan Publishing Co., Collier Books, 1955), p. 56.

2. Bernard of Clairvaux, A *Diary of Readings*, p. 56.

they have to accumulate things death only strips away. They go through life wearing spiritual blinders, always thinking horizontally, never lifting their eyes to see things from God's perspective.

Thankfully, in Luke 12:22–34, Jesus teaches us how to have that vertical view so that our energies can be spent on what really matters in life.

How Can We Live a Vertical Lifestyle?

Turning from the crowd (vv. 13–15), Jesus now addresses His disciples (v. 22a)—making a subtle but important point.

Only Disciples Can Live Vertically

Only a disciple of Christ is capable of living a vertical lifestyle. Why? Because it takes commitment, courage, and faithfulness. It takes a heart open to the Spirit's ways at the cost of getting our own way. Disciples devote themselves to growing in and being conformed to Christ's image. And as they mature, they learn to think and see and live like Him (see 1 Cor. 2:6–16).

We Must Cast Out Worry, Fear, and Selfishness

Worry, fear, and selfishness are our mortal foes. They keep us from seeking God first. They pin down our spirits and take our minds captive with horizontal thoughts. To break their power over us, Jesus confronts them, one by one.

1. *Worry.* Worry takes all the bad news on TV and puts us in the middle of it. Jesus, however, calmly takes our shaking hands in His and tells us not once, but twice:

> "For this reason I say to you, do not be anxious for your life, as to what you shall eat; nor for your body, as to what you shall put on. . . . Do not seek what you shall eat, and what you shall drink, and do not keep worrying." (Luke 12:22, 29)

Jesus uses two Greek words for this foe, translated in these verses *anxious* and *worrying*. The first is *merimnaō*, from a word meaning "to be divided, distracted."[3] The second is *meteorizō*, "to be tossed like a ship at sea . . . to be in doubt."[4] Worry often has two faces:

3. Archibald Thomas Robertson, *Word Pictures in the New Testament* (Grand Rapids, Mich.: Baker Book House, 1930), vol. 2, p. 156.

4. Robertson, *Word Pictures in the New Testament*, p. 177.

the distracted, bothered face of Martha, stewing and fussing in the kitchen (see 10:41); and the doubting, bewildered face of a person tossing and turning about the future.

Why do we wear these faces? Because, first, we fret about things that are not our responsibility. Jesus says we're not to worry about food and clothing, "for life is more than food, and the body than clothing" (12:23). It's God's responsibility, as our sustainer, to make sure we're fed and clothed.

Is Jesus saying we should neglect our jobs and simply wait for God to provide? No, but He's warning us against being obsessed with these things to the point of distraction.

How often have we just finished lunch and wondered, "What's for dinner?" We buy a new outfit and frown, "But what about next season?" Life is more than food and clothing. Jesus is telling us, "Take your minds off what it takes to live . . . and live!"

Second, we worry about things we cannot change or control. Jesus asks,

> "And which of you by being anxious can add a single cubit to his life's span? If then you cannot do even a very little thing, why are you anxious about other matters?" (vv. 25–26)

We can't add one second to our lives, much less a year. Neither can we alter the weather, the passing of time, people's reactions, or even the stock market! Yet how often we strain under these senseless bricks of worry.

To keep worry's load from flattening our perspective into a horizontal line, God has placed reminders of His provision for us all over His creation.

> "Consider the ravens, for they neither sow nor reap; and they have no storeroom nor barn; and yet God feeds them; how much more valuable you are than the birds! . . . Consider the lilies, how they grow; they neither toil nor spin; but I tell you, even Solomon in all his glory did not clothe himself like one of these. But if God so arrays the grass in the field, which is alive today and tomorrow is thrown into the furnace, how much more will He clothe you, O men of little faith!" (vv. 24, 27–28)

Are we so preoccupied with the cares of this world that we can't see how much God cares for His world? Listen to the message the birds sing as they splash in puddles and gather their seeds: "God provides for His own." Look with wonder at a hillside, and see what's written in the wildflowers: "God provides for His own."

If He cares for the raven and the lily, will He not provide for us, His children? Of course He will. So, Jesus says,

> "Do not seek what you shall eat, and what you shall drink, and do not keep worrying. For all these things the nations of the world eagerly seek; but your Father knows that you need these things. But seek for His kingdom, and these things shall be added to you." (vv. 29–31)

Here is the heart of Jesus' message: "Seek for His kingdom, and these things shall be added to you." *His* kingdom is preeminent, not ours. If we put His will first, we can count on His meeting our needs. Or as Spurgeon once put it, "You mind HIS business . . . He will mind yours."

2. *Fear*. In verse 22, Jesus said, "Do not be anxious." Now He says,

> "Do not be afraid, little flock, for your Father has chosen gladly to give you the kingdom." (v. 32)

Jesus doesn't ridicule us for our fears; He handles us with the kid gloves of grace, calling us "little flock." And note that our Father *gladly* gives us the kingdom. As James wrote,

> Every good thing bestowed and every perfect gift is from above, coming down from the Father of lights, with whom there is no variation, or shifting shadow. (James 1:17)

Why should He delight so in us? Because we're His children. He gives us what He would give His own Son. The world says we must earn favor, but God generously offers us what we need . . . and so much more.

3. *Selfishness*. Unchecked, worry and fear drive us straight into the hands of our third foe: selfishness. When this attitude invades our hearts, we become like the rich man in Jesus' parable, greedily laying up treasures for ourselves (Luke 12:21). We cling to our possessions as a person thrown overboard clutches pieces of floating debris. Once we realize that Christ has us in His grip, however, we're free to loosen our grasp on the things of this world. We're

ready to live by Jesus' command in verse 33:

> "Sell your possessions and give to charity; make yourselves purses which do not wear out, an unfailing treasure in heaven, where no thief comes near, nor moth destroys." (v. 33)

The Secret Lies in Our Hearts

Jesus concludes His lesson in vertical living with a principle that points to the heart of the matter.

> "For where your treasure is, there will your heart be also." (v. 34)

Where is your heart? Is your love buried in a bank vault? Is your joy printed on a business ledger? Is your life wrapped around your house and all the things in it? Or is your hope in heaven with Christ? Wherever you're stockpiling your treasure, that's where your heart will be.

What Must Change to Make Vertical Living Occur?

Life doesn't consist of our possessions. It consists of seeking God's kingdom, of filling our purses with celestial gold, of becoming rich toward God.

So how do we increase our heavenly treasure? First, *we have to change how we think before things happen.* We must say to ourselves, *I want God's will, not mine.* Then we'll see the situations in each day differently. We'll be able to find opportunities to display Christ's character and the qualities of His kingdom.

Also, *we must change how we react after things happen.* Most of us, by nature, react horizontally. We panic in the storm. We worry. We fear. We cling to possessions tightly. Instead, let's train ourselves to react vertically. No crash on Wall Street can depreciate the value of our heavenly assets. They're stored for us in God's vault, ready to pay us rich dividends the moment we step into glory.

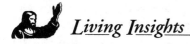

Living Insights — STUDY ONE

Let's delve more deeply into what Jesus meant when He instructed us to "seek for His kingdom." John Stott explains this all-encompassing command:

> God's kingdom is Jesus Christ ruling over his people in total blessing and total demand. To "seek first" this kingdom [Matt. 6:33] is to desire as of first importance the spread of the reign of Jesus Christ.[5]

God's kingdom always begins in our hearts and spreads outward to the world like ripples in a pond. The following diagram illustrates three realms in which we can pursue the reign of Christ.

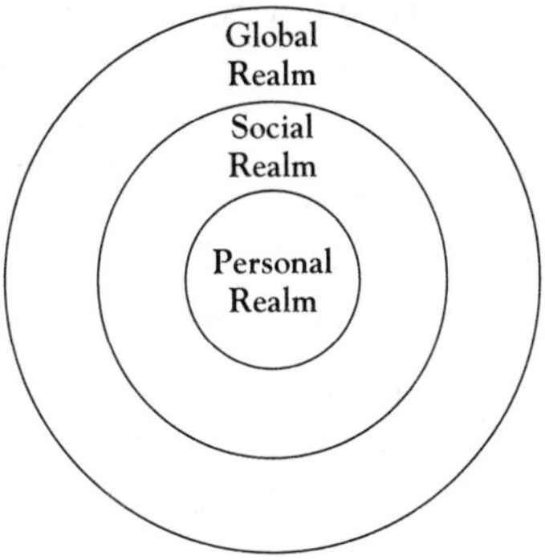

Take a quick survey of your personal realm. Do you see evidence of Christ's rule over your thoughts, your attitudes, your will? In this inner circle, what do you need to submit to Him?

____

____

____

____

Spilling out of our hearts, God's kingdom spreads to our next circle of influence: the social realm. Christ taught us to love our enemies (Luke 6:27–28), to treat people the way we want them to treat us (v. 31), to be merciful and generous (vv. 36–38), and to love our neighbors (10:25–37). How well are you submitting to Christ's rule as you relate to the people around you? What needs to change?

____

5. John R. W. Stott, *The Message of the Sermon on the Mount* (Matthew 5–7) rev. ed. of *Christian Counter-Culture* (Downers Grove, Ill.: InterVarsity Press, 1978), p. 170.

The farthest ripples of Christ's reign are felt all over the planet as we connect ourselves to the missionary challenge of the church (see Matt. 28:19–20). Besides giving donations, how can you get involved in spreading Christ's gospel to the world?

To spread the reign of Christ on earth is our highest calling. It is our purpose. "Life is more than food, and the body than clothing," Jesus said (Luke 12:23). It is seeking the kingdom of God in every area of our lives.

Living Insights — STUDY TWO

One news broadcast is enough to tie our stomachs in knots with worry. Listen to these fictional excerpts from a typical report:

> National debt skyrockets while the dollar nose-dives to post-war low. Some analysts say the economy may take years to recover . . .
>
> Major aerospace company announces plant closings in four cities. Thousands will be laid off . . .
>
> Violent crime spreads to once-quiet suburban haven as gunmen enter home and . . .
>
> Now for the weather. Showers locally, turning to thunderstorms later tonight. No end in sight to recent downpour . . .

Click.

Whew! I can feel my stomach tightening already. What will happen if the economy fails? Will I lose my job? How will we pay our bills? How will we keep food in the cupboards? How much do we have in savings?

> "All these things the nations of the world eagerly seek; but your Father knows that you need these things. But seek for His kingdom, and these things shall be added to you." (Luke 12:30–31)

What is the Lord telling you through these verses?

____

____

____

Remember, Christ is promoting trust, not carelessness. It's wise to plan ahead and provide for the needs of our families. But He doesn't want worry and fear to fester into selfishness and greed.

How does an attitude of trust help you obey Christ's command in verse 33?

____

____

____

How do you plan to build your treasure in heaven?

____

____

____

Do the newscasts make you wring your hands? Some would advise turning them off, but Christ has a better plan. Whenever the news—or anything else—starts to make you anxious, listen for the birds and look for the lilies. Their message of God's tender care for us can loosen the knots and put your mind at ease.

Chapter 10

LET'S BE READY FOR THE FUTURE

Luke 12:35–48

Hello? Hello, Sara!"

"Joe! Oh, Joe, is it really you?"

"Yes, baby, it's me! I'm in New York! I'm coming home on the first train out of here. The colonel told us it shouldn't be more than two days if—" the jubilant roar of fellow servicemen finally home from Europe crescendoed through cavernous Grand Central Station, drowning out Joe's voice.

"—then I'm home for good!" was all the rest that Sara caught. "I love you, baby!" Joe shouted into the receiver. "See you soon!"

"I love you too, honey! See you soon!" Then Sara sank down at the kitchen table, three years' worth of worrying, missing, hoping, and holding on finally released in grateful sobs.

She'd last felt Joe's arms around her on a soft spring day in 1942, as they said their good-byes before he was shipped overseas to England. They hadn't even been married a whole year yet, and he was gone. Out of her sight. Out of her reach. But never, *never* out of her heart. Three years of letters back and forth, of dreams of his return, of whispered prayers had only deepened her love for him. And now he was coming home!

"I've got to get ready!" Sara realized suddenly. She straightened the already-neat home, paid the Matlack boy down the street a dime to mow the lawn, restraightened what she'd just fixed, then tore it all apart in a frenzy of spring-cleaning. By the middle of the next day she had finished with that and set to work figuring out a proper homecoming meal.

"How many ration stamps have I saved up?" she wondered aloud. "Enough for a chicken dinner? Hmm, yes. And a chocolate cake—at least a small one. Oh, I can hardly wait till tomorrow!"

The next afternoon, the savory aroma of chicken and home-grown vegetables mingled with the cooling cake. After her tenth appraising look in the mirror and third change of clothes, Sara settled into arranging the daffodils Mrs. Carver had brought over.

"There, everything's ready. Now I just need Joe," she smiled softly.

Four hours later, her smile had faded. No Joe. When the clock struck one, Sara finally went to bed. The next day, she readied the house again. Still no Joe. The following day was the same, as was the day after that. On the sixth day after his phone call, Sara straightened the house once again, threw out the chicken salad (formerly the chicken dinner), replaced the nodding daffodils with a few newly blooming roses, and called the Matlack boy again.

Hanging up the phone, she turned toward the kitchen to figure out another meal. Then she saw him . . . still in uniform, hat in hand, silently watching her and smiling. And crying.

He was home for good.

The Immediate Concern on Jesus' Heart

"Be dressed in readiness," Jesus begins in this section of Luke 12, "and keep your lamps alight" (v. 35). Because at any moment, He can step through the door of history and return to us for good. As His bride, will we be eagerly waiting for Him? Will He find a ready home and a tender, welcoming heart?

Or will He return to an empty, run-down house, where people grew tired of waiting and moved somewhere else? Where the people He loved forgot all about Him?

Will He find joy? Or uneasy surprise?

Generally: Be Ready!

Jesus, of course, would rather find joy. Let's look again at His counsel in verse 35, so we can live in bright anticipation instead of trembling dread.

> "Be dressed in readiness, and keep your lamps alight."

In Greek, this verse begins with an emphatic use of the personal pronoun *you*. Jesus is talking to each of us: "You who worry and fear, you who cling to your fading possessions, *you*—make yourself ready. Take your eyes off the world and focus on Me."

So how can we do this? Jesus gives us two word pictures. First, in His day, when people "dressed in readiness" they gathered their outer robes and tucked them into their belts. Now they could travel or tend the horses or cook a meal unhindered. Their clothes revealed their ready-to-work mind-set—the same mind-set Jesus wants to see in us.

Jesus' second picture is in the command "Keep your lamps alight." In other words, keep the home fires burning. Even today, leaving a light on means someone is expected. It reveals a watchful, welcoming attitude. When Jesus returns, He doesn't want to arrive at a dark house while we yawn and fumble for the light switch. He wants to know that we've prepared a place for Him and are looking forward to His coming.

In the verses that follow, He uses two more elaborate analogies. The first is a wedding.

> "And be like men who are waiting for their master when he returns from the wedding feast, so that they may immediately open the door to him when he comes and knocks. Blessed are those slaves whom the master shall find on the alert when he comes; truly I say to you, that he will gird himself to serve, and have them recline at the table, and will come up and wait on them. Whether he comes in the second watch, or even in the third, and finds them so, blessed are those slaves." (vv. 36–38)

A Jewish wedding feast could last a week or more, so the servants deserved praise for watching and waiting, even through the night and early morning. This master, touched by their thoughtfulness, surprises them by wrapping a towel around his waist and becoming their servant. That's the way Jesus is, always returning our love with His love.

Jesus' second illustration has a more alarming tone:

> "And be sure of this, that if the head of the house had known at what hour the thief was coming, he would not have allowed his house to be broken into. You too, be ready; for the Son of Man is coming at an hour that you do not expect." (vv. 39–40)

Jesus is like the thief in the sense that He will break into our world without warning. Because we can't pinpoint the hour of His arrival, we have to be ready all the time. And the only way to *be* ready is to *keep* ready.

Now, what exactly does it mean to "keep ready"? Does Christ expect us to sit at home, anxiously wringing our hands and peering out the window? No, He wants us to get out and do His will in the world. He has plans for us while we wait, and accomplishing those plans is life's greatest adventure. It's a responsibility we can delight in.

Specifically: Be Responsible!

In response to a question Peter raises, Jesus tells us what we can expect as responsible stewards.

> And Peter said, "Lord, are You addressing this parable to us, or to everyone else as well?" And the Lord said, "Who then is the faithful and sensible steward, whom his master will put in charge of his servants, to give them their rations at the proper time? Blessed is that slave whom his master finds so doing when he comes. Truly I say to you, that he will put him in charge of all his possessions." (vv. 41–44)

The trustworthy steward proves himself worthy of more responsibilities in the future. For us that means that, if we are faithful, we will receive the rewards God has reserved for us in heaven.

However, the person who disregards God's will and does not live for the future will be like the irresponsible steward in verse 45.

> "But if that slave says in his heart, 'My master will be a long time in coming,' and begins to beat the slaves, both men and women, and to eat and drink and get drunk, the master of that slave will come on a day when he does not expect him, and at an hour he does not know, and will cut him in pieces, and assign him a place with the unbelievers." (v. 46)

As Jesus sketched this contemptible steward, He probably had in mind the false leaders of His day—the hypocrites who whipped the people with their rigid rules while they lounged around, drinking in their power. Because of the steward's arrogant cruelty, his punishment—and the punishment of all who follow his wicked example—will be swift and deadly.

But would Jesus literally cut someone into pieces? The point He is trying to get across is that the punishment will be severe. Unbelievers who have put off preparing their hearts for Jesus, who live as if life were a joke, will have something real to dread when Christ comes again. Not all unbelievers will bear such severe punishment, though. In the following verses, notice the different fates of those who know but neglect God's will and those who are ignorant of it.

> "And that slave who knew his master's will and did not get ready or act in accord with his will, shall receive many lashes, but the one who did not know it, and committed deeds worthy of a flogging, will receive but few." (vv. 47–48a)

Apparently, just as there are a variety of rewards in heaven, there are degrees of punishment in hell. God has given all people enough understanding of Himself to condemn them if they reject what they know (see Rom. 1:18–20). But if they have much knowledge and turn away, their judgment will be heavier than if they receive little and turn away.

> "And from everyone who has been given much shall much be required; and to whom they entrusted much, of him they will ask all the more." (Luke 12:48b)

The Indirect Connection to All Who Hear Jesus' Words

To whom much is given, much is required. With privilege comes responsibility. God has blessed us with more freedom and grace and knowledge than most people ever dream of having. It's tempting to enjoy our privileges and neglect our responsibilities. But God wants us to enjoy both. Knowing all we do about His coming can intimidate us, or it can thrill us and motivate us to get ready.

So let's put our houses in order. Let's lay out our best china for Him. Let's dress ourselves in the clothes He longs to see: "a heart of compassion, kindness, humility, gentleness, and patience" (Col. 3:12).

Let's be ready for when He comes to take us home for good.

Living Insights — STUDY ONE

While languishing in a Roman prison toward the end of his life, the apostle Paul would often peer past his cell's black walls into the brilliant expanse of heaven. The stench of the dungeon would fade as he inhaled the clear air of Paradise. His hard bed would soften as he reached out his arms to clutch the silken glory of Christ.

"I have fought the good fight," he wrote, "I have finished the course, I have kept the faith" (2 Tim. 4:7). His earthly epilogue was really a prologue to a new and wonderful future.

> In the future there is laid up for me the crown of righteousness, which the Lord, the righteous Judge, will award to me on that day; and not only to me, but also to all who have loved His appearing. (v. 8)

Are you, like Paul, one of those "who have loved His appearing"? How often do you think of Christ's return? How real does it seem to you?

Using Paul's prayer in Colossians 1:9–10 as a guide, how might your love for Jesus' appearing reveal itself in your life?

How might His second coming change your perspective toward the trials you endure (see 2 Cor. 4:8–10, 17–18)?

Of this we can be sure: the rose that is crushed today will, in His hands, bloom once again. As believers, we have hope. We look forward to a glorious future when we will never be apart from our Bridegroom again. We can endure the toughest prisons, as long as we can dream that dream.

Living Insights STUDY TWO

Perhaps the following prayer expresses your feelings after reading our Lord's words about His second coming. Circle any phrases that particularly touch you. And, if you'd like to, write a prayer in the space provided—your thoughts as a Bride waiting for her Groom.

Dear Jesus,

Someday, the sky will open and You will enter this world again. Forgive me for the times I misplaced the hope of that amid the bills and appointments and deadlines that clutter my days. Forgive me for the times I let the sparkle of the world steal my attention from the vision of Your glory.

Keep my eyes on You, Lord. Keep my heart yearning for the moment You open the door and enter my home. Keep my candle lit in the anticipation of seeing the beauty of Your face and hearing the tenderness in Your voice.

You have given me everything. To whom much is given, much is required. Help me to live to my potential.

Help me to keep my house in order, to not be satisfied with the bare walls of my life, but to decorate them with the things that appeal to You. An act of mercy. A word of encouragement. A tear of compassion.

Lord, may I dress to please You. May I clothe my body in purity, resisting the temptation to sell myself for untrue love. May I adorn my heart with fidelity, always keeping in mind the vow I made when You first came into my life.

Fire my soul with a desire for You. Help me never to lose my first love. Help me stay true to the end. Keep me vigilant through dark and desolate nights. Keep my candle lit, Lord. Please, keep my candle lit.

My Prayer

Chapter 11

LET'S BE REALISTIC ABOUT THE PRESENT

Luke 12:49–59

Thus says the Lord," Isaiah prophesied to mortally ill Hezekiah, "'Set your house in order, for you shall die and not live'" (Isa. 38:1).

A message like that would certainly put things in perspective, wouldn't it? And that's exactly what biblical prophecy is supposed to do—show us the whole story, the big picture of the beginning and the end, so we can "set our houses in order."

Some of us, however, become enthralled with prophecy in and of itself. We become so mesmerized by future events—the Rapture, the fiery end of the world, our ruling with Christ—that we're no good in the present. We get so focused on the Last Day that we become blind to *this* day.

Making us dull to present realities was never the prophets' intent. Nor was it Jesus'. His prophetic words to the disciples and the multitudes in this last section of Luke 12 provide a glimpse of what the end times will look like as well as some instructions on maintaining a proper perspective in the here and now.

To help us heed His message more clearly, let's first establish a framework for responding to God's prophetic word appropriately.

Inappropriate and Appropriate Reactions to Prophecy

Our response to prophecy can either sidetrack us into a wilderness wandering or spur us along the path of life.

Wrong Responses

At least three responses can lead us off track.

First, we can teeter on the edge of extremism and fanaticism: setting dates for world events and Jesus' return, building our theories on scant or nonexistent biblical evidence.

Second, we can stumble into thickets of theological dogmatism and argumentativeness: being open and teachable on everything but prophecy and fighting over different interpretations. If we're caught in this response, we won't budge to accommodate another opinion.

Third, we can wander in circles, making the study of prophecy an end in itself. We may spend hours fervently trying to match newspaper clippings with verses from the Bible. What good is all our figuring, however, if it never moves us one step forward in our walk with the Lord?

Whenever Scripture takes us to the future, it does so to give us a better view of the present and how we ought to live in light of what we know. Notice, for instance, Peter's fiery portrait of the judgment of the world.

> The present heavens and earth by His word are being reserved for fire, kept for the day of judgment and destruction of ungodly men. . . . The day of the Lord will come like a thief, in which the heavens will pass away with a roar and the elements will be destroyed with intense heat, and the earth and its works will be burned up. (2 Pet. 3:7, 10)

Yet he refuses to rest his pen until he draws the implication for our lives today:

> Since all these things are to be destroyed in this way, what sort of people ought you to be in holy conduct and godliness. . . .
>
> Be diligent to be found by Him in peace, spotless and blameless. (vv. 11, 14; see also 1 Thess. 4:13–5:11)

Viewing the future through God's prophetic telescope is supposed to change the way we look at the present. It is designed to rearrange our priorities and shape our values—today.

Right Responses

The wrong responses can easily sidetrack us, but the right responses can keep us on the road to growth. Let's look at the appropriate ways to view prophecy.

First, since prophecy is a part of God's revelation, it is obviously an important part of our spiritual curriculum. Prophetic themes resonate through Scripture, pouring forth anthems of the Lord's justice, His holiness, His mercy, His redemption. Listening to those powerful chords adds depth to our understanding of the melody of His love.

Second, we can look at prophecy as a continual reminder that God has a plan. He has everything under control, even when the world seems to be spinning off its axis. Rather than panicking, we can be strengthened to live a holy life for our almighty, omnipotent Lord.

And third, prophecy motivates us to share Christ, because it reminds us that we don't have forever to point our friends to Him.

The greater our awareness of Christ's second coming, the greater our desire to live for Him now. Future thinking guides present living—that's the lesson Jesus has for us in Luke 12.

Unrealistic and Realistic Views of the Present

Jesus' picture of the future and the coming kingdom of God skewers several popular misconceptions about this earth, Jesus' own mission, and world peace. Let's listen attentively as He sets the record straight.

Popular but Incorrect Ideas

1. *About this earth.* Today the popular thinking is that the earth is sacred, the "mother" of all life. We must care for it so it will last forever, right? Wrong. Jesus' shocking opening statement obliterates this idea:

> "I have come to cast fire upon the earth; and how I wish it were already kindled!"[1] (Luke 12:49)

Peter has already told us that "the earth and its works will be burned up" in judgment (2 Pet. 3:10). There is nothing that is permanent, then, except the eternal souls of human beings and God's everlasting Word.

Jesus is referring to the time when God's plan will have run its course—when all the pain, all the heartache, all the disasters, all the calamities, all the consequences of sin will be finished. When it's all over, when judgment's done, when the family of God will be united in peace. Jesus longed to fulfill His role as Judge because that would signal the death of sin and the dawn of the new heavens and the new earth.

1. William Barclay explains why this verse jolted the Jewish listeners of Jesus' day: "They regarded the Messiah as conqueror and king, and the Messianic age as a golden time. In Jewish thought fire is almost always the symbol of *judgment*. So, then, Jesus regarded the coming of his kingdom as a time of judgment. The Jews firmly believed that God would judge other nations by one standard and themselves by another; that the very fact that a man was a Jew would be enough to absolve him." *The Gospel of Luke*, rev. ed., The Daily Study Bible Series (Philadelphia, Pa.: Westminster Press, 1975), p. 169.

Remember, He holds the blueprints for another world, a grander place that He has designed for us. As Peter wrote: "We are looking for new heavens and a new earth, in which righteousness dwells" (2 Pet. 3:13). Although we must be wise stewards and have respect for the work of God's hands, this earth is not the paradise God has planned.

2. *About Jesus' mission.* Some people believe Jesus came to subdue the world with a philosophy of love, but that the forces of hate overwhelmed Him and killed Him. The Cross, therefore, symbolizes the tragic end of Christ's impossible dream. However, the Cross was no mistake; it was the centerpiece of Jesus' mission.

> "But I have a baptism to undergo, and how distressed I am until it is accomplished!" (Luke 12:50)

This "baptism" would be no dip in the Jordan river, but an immersion in the fiery cauldron of God's wrath. Jesus came to suffer God's judgment so that we might avoid it (see John 3:16–17). The Cross symbolizes spiritual victory, not defeat. It is the bridge of peace joining sinful people and a holy God.

3. *About peace.* Another popular but incorrect idea is that our human power can establish peace in the world. It's a noble aim, but an unrealistic and even misguided one. Even Jesus didn't come to establish world peace. On the contrary, He frequently disrupted it!

> "Do you suppose that I came to grant peace on earth? I tell you, no, but rather division; for from now on five members in one household will be divided, three against two, and two against three. They will be divided, father against son, and son against father; mother against daughter, and daughter against mother; mother-in-law against daughter-in-law, and daughter-in-law against mother-in-law." (Luke 12:51–53)

Just because the angels rejoice when a soul is saved doesn't mean that sinful human beings will have the sense to do the same. For example, a believing spouse who desires to follow the Lord may have conflict with an unbelieving spouse who has no interest in serving Christ. The two will never be completely one because they have each pledged their allegiance to different things. William Barclay has said,

> The essence of Christianity is that loyalty to Christ

> has to take precedence over the dearest loyalties of this earth.[2]

Remember, Christ offers us peace with God, not peace with the world. Nor, necessarily, peace with our families. The more we live as citizens of His kingdom, the more disharmony we can expect between us and the citizens of this earth.

Rare but Needed Reproofs

Having blown the fog of misperception away, Jesus now awakens our dull minds with a couple of sharp reproofs.

First, *we fail to analyze the present time in which we live.*

> And He was also saying to the multitudes, "When you see a cloud rising in the west, immediately you say, 'A shower is coming,' and so it turns out. And when you see a south wind blowing, you say, 'It will be a hot day,' and it turns out that way. You hypocrites! You know how to analyze the appearance of the earth and the sky, but why do you not analyze this present time?" (vv. 54–56)

Although we can tell when a rainstorm or a tornado is coming, we too often ignore the signs of the times. The multitudes of Christ's day were much the same. If they had only held their finger to the breeze swirling around Jesus' ministry, they would have sensed that the Son of Salvation was shining brightly . . . and that judgment was in the wind. The writer to the Hebrews rounds out Jesus' statement with some practical counsel:

> "Today if you hear His voice,
> Do not harden your hearts." (Heb. 4:7b)

Instead, we should soften our hearts toward God and each other, as Jesus' next reproof makes clear: *We fail to solve our personal squabbles correctly.*

> "And why do you not even on your own initiative judge what is right? For while you are going with your opponent to appear before the magistrate, on your way there make an effort to settle with him, in

2. Barclay, *The Gospel of Luke*, p. 170.

order that he may not drag you before the judge, and the judge turn you over to the constable, and the constable throw you into prison. I say to you, you shall not get out of there until you have paid the very last cent." (Luke 12:57–59)

How quick we are today to drag each other to court—even Christians with other Christians! Jesus says, "Settle now!" And in the grander scheme of things, He tells us to settle our debt of sin before we stand before our Judge. For if we wait until He hears our case, it will be too late for Christ to intercede.

Extreme and Balanced Responses in Our Personal Lives

How, then, do we respond to Christ's prophetic words? An extreme response would be to live completely for the future: quit our jobs, sell our possessions, and separate ourselves from unbelievers. And since there's no chance for peace, give up trying to make the world a better place.

A more balanced response is to live joyously now, while anticipating the future. Christ revealed the end times to motivate us in the present times. His coming compels us to share the gospel more urgently, to serve Him more faithfully, and to give ourselves to others more freely.

In closing, here are a couple of tips to help you keep in mind what Jesus has been teaching. First, whenever you see the word *peace*, whether on a banner or in the news, remember that, until Christ returns, true peace on earth can only occur within a person's heart. Second, the next time you hear a weather forecast based on the signs in the sky, remember to read the signs of the times. Jesus could appear at any moment—with the next change in the wind or the next cloud on the horizon.

Living Insights STUDY ONE

Are you sure that you will pass safely through God's judgment fire? You can be. Read the following verses, and write down what Christ has done to provide you safe passage.

- Isaiah 53:5–6 ______________________________

____

- Romans 5:8–9 ________________________________

____

- 1 Thessalonians 5:9–10 ________________________

____

According to 1 Peter 1:3–5, what has God done for you?

____

____

____

What role does the Holy Spirit play (see Eph. 1:13–14)?

____

____

If you have trusted Christ for your salvation, you are shielded by the Father, Son, and Holy Spirit—three layers of divine, fireproof protection.

Do you sometimes wonder whether that is enough? In what ways does God's future judgment frighten you?

____

____

____

Jude concludes his brief epistle with a benediction that was written with you in mind. Write your name in the blanks below to personalize God's promise to you. And rest in the assurance of your salvation.

> Now to Him who is able to keep ____________ from stumbling, and to make ____________ stand in the presence of His glory blameless with great joy, to the only God, ____________'s Savior, through Jesus Christ, ____________'s Lord, be glory, majesty, dominion and authority, before all time and now and forever. Amen. (see vv. 24–25)

Living Insights STUDY TWO

Christ could return at any moment. He might come before the sun rises on your plans for tomorrow, or before you turn out the lights and climb into bed. Or before you close this book.

In light of His imminent appearing, how should we live? What does Scripture say?

- Romans 13:11–14 ______________________________

- Philippians 4:4–5 ______________________________

- James 5:7–9 ______________________________

- 1 Peter 4:7 ______________________________

Knowing that Christ is coming shuffles our priorities. The things that last for eternity take on greater importance than the things that will be left behind. Based on the verses you just read and your personal feelings about Christ's return, what life priorities do you need to bring to the top of your stack?

What can you do this week to live out this reordering?

Chapter 12

What a Difference Jesus Makes!

Luke 13:1–17

There is a simple wood carving that beautifully depicts the hope of Christianity. It portrays Jesus' hand, upright and cupped, with a person nestled in His palm. The carving reminds us of our security in Christ and His precious promise:

> "I give eternal life to them, and they shall never perish; and no one shall snatch them out of My hand." (John 10:28)

Imagine, though, what life would be like without Christ to hold us. Without His assurance of heaven. Without His comforting hand around our lives.

Suppose you've just had a tumor removed and the doctor is reading you the biopsy report. The news isn't good. The most vicious type of cancer has invaded your body. As the doctor describes the tortuous road ahead for you, fear grips your soul. Without Christ, who will soothe your inner pain and walk with you through this cold, dark valley?

Or let's say that, after twenty-five years of marriage, your spouse announces, "I've been seeing someone else. I don't love you anymore. I want a divorce." An emotional hailstorm of confusion, anger, grief, and guilt crashes around you. Who can you run to for comfort during the long and anguished nights to come? Without Christ, there is no one.

What a difference Jesus makes! It's not that He shields our hearts from pain—sorrow strikes everyone. It's that He gives us Himself through the pain. And, as we'll see in our passage, He brings us three priceless treasures: His perspective when tragedy strikes, His patience when we fail, and His freedom when we're in bondage.

The Difference Jesus Makes

First, Jesus shows us His unique perspective on life's tragedies.

In His Teaching

The finest teacher who ever lived, Jesus clips two tragic stories from the local newspaper and uses them as illustrations to drive home an important point about repentance.

> Now on the same occasion there were some present who reported to Him about the Galileans, whose blood Pilate had mingled with their sacrifices. And He answered and said to them, "Do you suppose that these Galileans were greater sinners than all other Galileans, because they suffered this fate? I tell you, no, but, unless you repent, you will all likewise perish. Or do you suppose that those eighteen on whom the tower in Siloam fell and killed them, were worse culprits than all the men who live in Jerusalem? I tell you, no, but unless you repent, you will all likewise perish." (Luke 13:1–5)

No other historian but Luke records the two events Jesus describes here. Both stories, according to William Barclay, may be related to a well-documented plan of Pilate's to improve Jerusalem's aqueduct system using temple funds. The idea of dipping into God's treasury for a city works project enraged the Jews, and mobs gathered at the temple in protest. Barclay explains what happened when Pilate sent disguised soldiers into the crowd.

> At a given signal they were to fall on the mob and disperse them. This was done, but the soldiers dealt with the mob with a violence far beyond their instructions and a considerable number of people lost their lives. Almost certainly Galileans would be involved in that.[1]

Apparently, a group of Galileans were sacrificing at the altar when the soldiers attacked them, for Jesus adds the grim detail that their blood was "mingled with their sacrifices."

The incident of the tower falling may also be related to Pilate's building project. Barclay points out that the word translated *culprits* can mean *debtors*. "Maybe we have a clue here," he writes.

1. William Barclay, *The Gospel of Luke*, rev. ed., The Daily Study Bible Series (Philadelphia, Pa.: Westminster Press, 1975), p. 173.

> It has been suggested that they had actually taken work on Pilate's hated aqueducts. If so, any money they earned was due to God and should have been voluntarily handed over, because it had already been stolen from him; and it may well be that popular talk had declared that the tower had fallen on them because of the work they had consented to do.[2]

In the Jewish mind, nothing happened by chance. Roman soldiers didn't murder some and spare others, nor did towers fall on some people and not on others for no reason. God dealt life's cards according to what we deserved. To good people, He dealt wealth and comforts; to bad people, tragedy and death. Therefore, according to the Jews, the ones who died must have been worse sinners than the ones who lived.

Onto this black-and-white theology of suffering, Jesus splashed the colors of a new perspective of grace. Because we're all sinners to God, salvation depends on repentance, not on who's better than whom. When tragedies fall on us, we may feel like God is punishing us, but He's really not. Remember Christ's perspective in verses 1 through 5. No matter what may crush us in this life, we know that the final tragedy, eternal death, cannot steal us away from Him (see Rom. 8:35–39). With Christ, our future is secure.

In His Timing

Of course, many claim to have repented, to belong to Christ. But those who have genuinely repented should, as John the Baptizer said, "bear fruits in keeping with repentance" (Luke 3:8). Yet even in this issue Christ offers us grace upon grace.

> And He began telling this parable: "A certain man had a fig tree which had been planted in his vineyard; and he came looking for fruit on it, and did not find any. And he said to the vineyard-keeper, 'Behold, for three years I have come looking for fruit on this fig tree without finding any. Cut it down! Why does it even use up the ground?' And he answered and said to him, 'Let it alone, sir, for this year too, until I dig around it and put in fertilizer;

2. Barclay, *The Gospel of Luke*, p. 173.

> and if it bears fruit next year, fine; but if not, cut it down.'" (13:6–9)

Even when we fail to produce the fruit that our divine landowner has expected us to bear, Jesus gives us time. He patiently cultivates our roots, allowing us room to grow. He sprinkles the fertilizer of His Word on the ground around us, inviting us to absorb His life-changing principles. Then He watches and waits for His Word to bloom and bear fruit.

But He can't wait forever. "It is appointed for men to die once and after this comes judgment" (Heb. 9:27). There is a limit to the time we have on earth to show God our fruit. In His eyes, unless we bear fruit, we haven't truly repented; and without repentance, we have no hope of eternal life.

In His Touch

Third, the touch of Christ makes a difference in our lives. Luke sketches this point on the canvas of Scripture with a vivid story about Jesus freeing a woman from a crippling evil spirit.

> And He was teaching in one of the synagogues on the Sabbath. And behold, there was a woman who for eighteen years had had a sickness caused by a spirit; and she was bent double, and could not straighten up at all. (Luke 13:10–11)

For eighteen years, the devilish spirit had been bending her spine like an iron bar, hunching her over and pressing her face downward. As she hobbled to the synagogue that day, all she could see was the dirt and gravel at her feet. That was her world. No one could help her; perhaps, no one even cared. But with eyes of compassion, Jesus noticed her bent shape in the crowd.

> He called her over and said to her, "Woman, you are freed from your sickness." And He laid His hands upon her; and immediately she was made erect again, and began glorifying God. (vv. 12–13)

With one touch, Jesus unclenched her knotted muscles and softened her calcified bones. In an instant, the woman blossomed like a rosebud. She lifted her face to the Sun of life and stretched her arms to the sky in praise to God.

But what put a smile on the Lord's face put a scowl on the face of a certain synagogue official, who clapped his rule book over the service to bring it under control.

> And the synagogue official, indignant because Jesus had healed on the Sabbath, began saying to the multitude in response, "There are six days in which work should be done; therefore come during them and get healed, and not on the Sabbath day." (v. 14)

Legalism smothers spontaneity. It confines God to a box and tells Him what He can and cannot do. It values rules more than the people the rules were meant to serve. The official should have been joining hands with the liberated woman in celebration. Instead, he was putting her back in bondage.

Jesus turned to the man and his nodding supporters, who were simmering together in their piety, and said:

> "You hypocrites, does not each of you on the Sabbath untie his ox or his donkey from the stall, and lead him away to water him? And this woman, a daughter of Abraham as she is, whom Satan has bound for eighteen long years, should she not have been released from this bond on the Sabbath day?" (vv. 15–16)

His questions turned up the heat, boiling these legalists in their own pot of rules. Did they really value donkeys more than people? Was that true?

> And as He said this, all His opponents were being humiliated; and the entire multitude was rejoicing over all the glorious things being done by Him. (v. 17)

When the hand of Christ touches a person, the results are nothing short of glorious. He loosens Satan's grip. He straightens what sin has bent. He frees us from the bonds of legalism.

What a difference Jesus makes!

Conclusion

Has Jesus made a difference in your life? Maybe something He taught has penetrated the confusion in your heart. Perhaps His timing in a certain situation has affirmed your confidence in His love for you. Or possibly you've felt His healing touch straighten a bent area of your life. If so, cherish these memories. Each experience with Christ on earth is a precious treasure—a foretaste of the spectacular glory that awaits you when you see Him face to face.

Living Insights STUDY ONE

Grandmother once stood straight, a long time ago, in the spring of her life. Her body was like the stem of a tulip, and the long braids that curled around her head were like golden petals. She was a beautiful woman.

But the years lay heavy on her shoulders, and the osteoporosis made her bones soft and melt together. Each time I saw her, I had to bend lower and lower to kiss her.

By her ninetieth birthday, her long braids were salty white, and her body had become shriveled and stooped. She shuffled when she walked. Her head bowed forward, and she had to crane her neck to look up at me. How I wished Jesus would touch my grandmother's bent little body and make it bloom again.

Are you struggling because Jesus hasn't touched the back of someone you love? Are you fearful because your own back is showing signs of weakness and decline? Read 1 Thessalonians 4:16–18 and 1 Corinthians 15:51–55. What will happen to our bodies when Jesus returns?

What is the hardest part about waiting for that resurrection day?

To all the bent-over women, to all the stooped people who must bear a heavy load of physical disabilities, to everyone whom Jesus hasn't touched yet, don't lose hope. One day, you'll close your eyes and awake to His loving touch. One day, even your body will bloom eternal.

Living Insights STUDY TWO

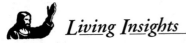

More than anything else, what is God looking for in our lives? Spiritual fruit. Take a moment to jot down the fruit of the Spirit that Paul lists in Galatians 5:22–23.

____

____

____

That's the kind of fruit Jesus hoped to see in the Jews, but for too long they had planted their lives in the cracked, hard ground of legalism. How do you think an obsession with rules keeps a person from bearing the fruit you listed above?

____

____

____

In what ways do you think Jesus breaks up this dry, legalistic soil? Note how He broke up the legalism in Paul's life (see 1 Timothy 1:12–16).

____

____

____

If you're rooted in legalism, open your heart to Christ's love. Absorb His mercy into your life, and watch the fruit grow.

Chapter 13

STRAIGHT TALK FOR SAINTS AND SINNERS

Luke 13:18–35

When designing an advertising campaign for a new bath soap, an ad manager asked his staff to analyze what made the product different from the rest. One clerk turned in the following answer:

> "The alkaline elements and vegetable fats in this product are blended in such a way as to secure the highest quality of saponification alone, with a specific gravity that keeps it on top of the water, relieving the bather of the trouble and annoyance of fishing around for it in the bottom during his ablutions."
>
> The advertising manager blue-penciled this and substituted the two words, "It floats."[1]

Ahhh, the power of simple words. We don't need long, convoluted sentences to tell us what we want to know. We like our communication crisp. Bite-sized. Chewable.

That's how Jesus spoke. The Jewish sophisticates heaped mounds of confusing religious verbiage on the people. But Jesus cut to the heart. His messages were profound yet plain. He spoke about the things that really matter: life, death, God, heaven. Jesus trimmed the fat and gave us the facts. Just the way we like it.

Straight Talk about the Kingdom

In our passage, Jesus first talks straight about the kingdom of God, a subject dear to the heart of every first-century Jew.

The setting is the synagogue, in which Jesus has just healed the stooped-over woman and exposed the hypocrisy of the religious leaders. An electric enthusiasm courses through the room, as the people rejoice over "the glorious things" He is doing (Luke 13:10–17).

Perhaps their conversation centered on the idea that this must

1. As quoted by Paul Lee Tan, comp., *Encyclopedia of 7,700 Illustrations: Signs of the Times* (Chicago, Ill.: Assurance Publishers, 1979), p. 115.

be what the kingdom of God would be like, for Jesus responds with two parables illustrating the true nature of the kingdom. It is unlike anything they could have imagined.

Jesus pauses, pondering a way to clear the fog. "What is the kingdom of God like, and to what shall I compare it?" (v. 18b). And again, "To what shall I compare the kingdom of God?" (v. 20).

An analogy comes to His mind drawn not from the great empires of the past but from the soil of their own backyards.

"Like a Mustard Seed"

> "It is like a mustard seed, which a man took and threw into his own garden; and it grew and became a tree; and the birds of the air nested in its branches." (v. 19)

"Small as a mustard seed" was a common expression used by the rabbis to describe something minute, "such as the least drop of blood . . . or the smallest remnant of sun-glow in the sky."[2] Jesus was saying, to the surprise of His audience, that God's kingdom begins as something insignificant—a seed tiny enough to get lost in the palm of your hand. Then it grows. And grows. And grows! It becomes a tree, large enough for birds to nest in its branches.[3]

Looking back on the history of the church, we've seen this incredible growth, haven't we? Within forty years of the Resurrection, the roots of the gospel had dug keep into the major centers of the Roman empire. Today, the tree continues to stretch its branches over walls and across borders, providing a spiritual nesting place for people of every culture in the world.

"Like Leaven"

To illustrate *how* the kingdom grows, Jesus leads us out of the garden and into the kitchen:

> "It is like leaven, which a woman took and hid in three pecks of meal, until it was all leavened." (v. 21)

Unlike the kingdoms of the world that grow by external force, Christ's reign works internally. It penetrates us like yeast permeates

2. Alfred Edersheim, *The Life and Times of Jesus the Messiah* (Mclean, Va.: Macdonald Publishing Co., 1886), vol. 1, book 3, pp. 592–93.

3. In a dream, Nebuchadnezzar envisioned his kingdom as a tree, in which "the birds of the sky dwelt in its branches" (Dan. 4:12). God's kingdom will be like his, only far greater.

dough. It begins with a spoonful of grace stirred into our lives, changing our attitudes and influencing our actions. One by one, individuals are transformed, then families, then churches, then communities. No other kingdom on earth can change people and societies the way Christ's can.

Straight Talk about Salvation

Who will enter God's kingdom? Jesus gives us the straight answer to this question later, while traveling to Jerusalem.

Are Just a Few Being Saved?

> And He was passing through from one city and village to another, teaching, and proceeding on His way to Jerusalem. And someone said to Him, "Lord, are there just a few who are being saved?" (vv. 22–23a)

According to the rabbis, all Israel would enter the kingdom, except for a few hardened sinners. But this person had apparently listened to Jesus long enough for a different idea to begin to dawn. And with perception Jesus includes His answer to the question of "how many" with His answer to a much more significant question: "*How?*"

> "Strive to enter by the narrow door; for many, I tell you, will seek to enter and will not be able." (v. 24)

According to Jesus, there is only one entrance to the kingdom of God—faith in Jesus Himself. Many people object to this idea. "Surely there are as many ways to God as there are individuals," they protest.

Yet think of the situations in life that require things to be done in a certain way. To board an airplane, we must have the right ticket. To enter a foreign country, we must show an official passport. And none of us would consider the airline or the government narrow-minded. We acknowledge readily their right—even their necessity—to set requirements of passage. Why, then, would we deny God the same privilege?

Because we want God's kingdom, but on our own terms. Jesus says we have to "strive," literally *agonize*, to enter this door—which means we can't come our way, we must come God's way. We'd like to open the door wide enough to let in anyone who is generally good or sincere, wide enough to offer benign tolerance of many personal philosophies. But Christ won't do so.

Merciful—God is that. Compassionate, patient—yes, that too. But on this one point, He is absolutely unbending. We are all sinners, deserving of eternal separation from our perfect and holy God. Yet in His grace, He has offered us a way of salvation—*one* way—in the substitutionary death of His Son, Jesus. Through that one door may we enter His kingdom.

And one day, even that door will be closed.

Do People Have Forever to Be Saved?

Jesus warns us what will happen when that day arrives.

> "Once the head of the house gets up and shuts the door, and you begin to stand outside and knock on the door, saying, 'Lord, open up to us!' then He will answer and say to you, I do not know where you are from.' Then you will begin to say, 'We ate and drank in Your presence, and You taught in our streets'; and He will say, 'I tell you, I do not know where you are from; depart from Me, all you evildoers.' There will be weeping and gnashing of teeth there when you see Abraham and Isaac and Jacob and all the prophets in the kingdom of God, but yourselves being cast out." (vv. 25–28)

Thousands of Jews had eaten bread with Jesus, but only a few had eaten the Bread of Life He offered. Thousands had heard Him speak in their streets, but only a few had taken His words to heart. Knowing about Christ is not the same as believing in Him. And whoever doesn't believe in Him will be locked out of the kingdom.

Will There Be Surprises in Heaven?

The door may be narrow, but the good news is that it is open to anyone. The Jews assumed they had a reserved seat in God's kingdom just because they were the children of Abraham. But God doesn't measure us by our bloodlines, wealth, or status . . . only by our faith. And those who think they are first on the guest list may be surprised to find their names at the bottom.

> "And they will come from east and west, and from north and south, and will recline at the table in the kingdom of God. And behold, some are last who

will be first and some are first who will be last."[4] (vv. 29–30)

Straight Talk about His Mission

Jesus came to earth with this all-consuming mission in mind: to provide a way for us to enter God's kingdom. No one, not even the most powerful of kings, could deter Him from His goal.

His Plan Will Not Be Hindered

> Just at that time some Pharisees came up, saying to Him, "Go away and depart from here, for Herod wants to kill You." And He said to them, "Go and tell that fox, 'Behold, I cast out demons and perform cures today and tomorrow, and the third day I reach My goal.' Nevertheless I must journey on today and tomorrow and the next day; for it cannot be that a prophet should perish outside of Jerusalem." (vv. 31–33)

Herod may have thought he was a lion, roaring threateningly. But to Jesus, he was nothing more than a skittish fox.

If you take your orders from the King of Kings, do not fear earthly kings, no matter how loudly they may roar. If God has given you a mission, He will see you through to the end.

His Offer Is Forced on No One

Jerusalem and a cruel cross lay at the end of Jesus' road. Yet He was not bitter. From His veins would pour the blood of a compassionate heart.

> "O Jerusalem, Jerusalem, the city that kills the prophets and stones those sent to her! How often I wanted to gather your children together, just as a hen gathers her brood under her wings, and you would not have it! Behold, your house is left to you desolate; and I say to you, you shall not see Me until the time comes when you say, 'Blessed is He who comes in the name of the Lord!'" (vv. 34–35)

4. This verse suggests that, just as there are degrees of punishment in hell (see Luke 12:41–48), there are degrees of rewards in heaven.

He still longs to gather people under His wings, and people still reject Him. He forces His offer of salvation on no one, yet He dreads the desolation they will endure at His return. On that day, they will see Him for who He is, the Son of God, the narrow door. But by then, it will be too late.

Straight Talk to All Who Hear

Jesus gives it to us straight and clear: the reality of death is sure, the way to God is through Christ alone, the time to decide is now.

Have you trusted Him for your salvation? He longs to welcome you into His kingdom. But He won't force you. You must come to Him on your own, through the narrow door.

Living Insights — STUDY ONE

We may not like to admit it, but we are all living in a house on fire. Time and age are slowly consuming us, and one day, all our timbers will be spent and our buildings will collapse in ashes. We don't like to talk about it, but Jesus keeps bringing up the subject . . . because He wants to show us the way of escape.

Have you walked through that narrow door?

For the gateway to a kingdom, it's hardly ostentatious. In fact, it's as mundane and homely as a stable entrance and as unappealing as the dark, dark opening of a tomb. Yet it's the only way in. And beyond it waits the wealth and treasure of the Father's love, vast, unlimited, *yours*—when you pass through that door. Won't you step toward it now? The battle with your intellect, your ego, your guilt may be agonizing, but at the slightest touch of your hand, the door will be flung open, and God's peace will flood your soul. In this chapter, we've offered you straight talk about salvation. Perhaps it's time you gave Jesus a straight answer.

If the answer you decided on was yes, perhaps this simple prayer can guide your response.

> *Dear Jesus:*
>
> *You know that I'm a sinner. You shed your blood on the cross and died to provide me a way to have eternal*

life with You. I believe in You. I believe that God has forgiven my sins because of what You've done for me. I step through this narrow door of faith, trusting You with my life. You are my only way to salvation. Thank you for receiving me into Your kingdom. Amen.

If you entered Christ's kingdom just now, won't you write us and tell us about it? We have a staff of counselors who would love to encourage you in your new journey with the Lord. Write to: Insight for Living, Counseling Department, Post Office Box 69000, Anaheim, California 92817-0900.

Living Insights — STUDY TWO

These days, some Christians seem to be more preoccupied with toppling corrupt political systems than transforming hearts. Yet when Jesus was on earth, He focused on people, not issues. Ken Gire notes:

> Oddly, Jesus addresses none of the pressing issues that plagued the first century. The government was godless, yet he led no revolt to overthrow it. The populace was heavily taxed, yet he led no rally for economic reform. Many of the people were slaves, yet he led no movement to liberate them. Poverty. Classism. Racism. The list of social ills was as long as it was ugly.
>
> Instead of making that list his political agenda, Jesus was content to plant the tiniest of seeds in the unlikeliest soil, to hide a lump of grace in the life of a nobody.
>
> A fisherman. A tax collector. A centurion.
>
> Heart by heart that's the way the kingdom of God grew. Quietly reaching for the sun. Spreading throughout history so people from every tribe and nation could one day roost in its branches.[5]

Didn't Jesus care about the godless government and about the

5. Ken Gire, *Instructive Moments with the Savior* (Grand Rapids, Mich.: Zondervan Publishing House, 1992), p. 84.

oppressive slave system? Of course He did. But He knew that the best way to change society was to change people. It's the "leaven" principle. In what ways is God's leaven transforming your life?

____

____

____

____

Would you like to see Christ transform someone you know? Who is that person? What can you do to tuck a lump of His grace into his or her heart?

____

____

____

Put the leaven principle into action wherever you go. Who can say what lives you'll touch . . . maybe a future business leader, professor, or president!

Chapter 14

SPIRITUAL TABLE MANNERS

Luke 14:1–24

Have you noticed that one of the best times for learning is mealtime? Sharing food together breaks down barriers and starts meaningful conversations. A professor, for example, can teach passionately in a lecture hall and inspire little more reaction than a few sleepy nods. But put those students around the same professor in a dining hall, and they're asking questions, chewing on issues, and gulping down concepts faster than he can dish them out.

Jesus, the consummate teacher, certainly seems to have understood this concept. Just think how many of the significant lessons in Luke—and the other gospels—took place over a banquet table or at a hillside picnic.

Mealtimes: A Great Place to Learn

For instance, do you know where He performed His first miracle? At a wedding feast in Cana (John 2:1–11). And what about the time He took the little boy's loaves and fishes and turned them into lunch for five thousand (Luke 9:10–17)? And then there's His memorable moment in Martha's kitchen, when He turned down the heat under her boiling frustration and offered her a cool sip of His peace (Luke 10:38–42). Then later, at the same house, He gave a lesson on the value of costly worship when Mary anointed His feet with perfume—during a meal (John 12:2–8).

And who could forget the most famous meal in the gospels, the Last Supper (John 13–17). Gathered around that table, the disciples surely savored every morsel Jesus served. It was a feast of unforgettable lessons in servanthood, leadership, abiding in Christ, loving one another, the Holy Spirit, and the future. The nourishment of that meal would have to last them through the lean, hungry, and horrible days ahead until after His resurrection, when they would eat with Jesus again on the shore of Galilee and witness His encouragement of Simon Peter (John 21).

Looking into the future, we see another meal—the glorious "marriage supper of the Lamb" (Rev. 19:7–9). On that day, we'll be dressed as Christ's perfect bride in the bright and clean linen of righteousness. We'll join Him in a celestial celebration that will last forever. What a meal that will be!

The stories go on and on.

So when we find Jesus in Luke 14 sitting down for dinner, we're not surprised that He takes this setting as an opportunity to serve up some memorable lessons—lessons that we're calling "spiritual table manners."

Jesus Ministers around the Table

In the first verse, Luke raises the curtain on a four-act play to follow. Jesus has entered the house of "one of the leaders of the Pharisees" (Luke 14:1a). This man is probably a member of the Sanhedrin, the elite ruling body of the Jews that will later convict Jesus of blasphemy (Matt. 26:63–66).

Foreshadowing the last week of Jesus' life, this religious leader and his preselected jury of Pharisees are already standing in judgment over Jesus. It is the Sabbath and they are "watching him closely" (Luke 14:1b). Literally, the Greek phrase means that they are "watching on the side (on the sly), watching insidiously, with evil intent."[1]

Through narrow eyes, they scrutinize His every move, ready to jump to a guilty verdict the moment He trips over a Sabbath law.

God had created the Sabbath as a day of rest, a time for refreshment in the green meadows of His presence. But the legalists had turned the Sabbath into a jungle of overgrown regulations. That's the nature of legalism. It finds us running free in the open spaces of God's grace and entangles us in so many rules that we can't move. It makes fearful what God created for joy, and Jesus will have none of it—then or now.

Rebuking the Legalists

The first scene opens with the introduction of a diseased man and a not-so-subtle challenge from the Pharisees.

> And there, in front of Jesus was a certain man suffering from dropsy. (v. 2)

Dropsy—today we call it edema—causes the victim's body to swell grotesquely and often indicates a serious kidney, liver, blood,

1. Archibald Thomas Robertson, *The Gospel according to Luke*, from *Word Pictures in the New Testament*, vol. 2 (Grand Rapids, Mich.: Baker Book House, 1930), p. 194.

or heart condition. Adding to the suffering, the rabbis attached a social stigma to the disease—to them, the disease was the bitter fruit of a grievous sin in the person's life.[2]

It's not hard to guess who probably staged this scene. The Pharisees knew that Jesus' compassionate heart would break for this suffering man, and He would want to heal him. But it wasn't sympathy that moved the Pharisees to position him right in front of Jesus. They were using him to bait a trap. The Lord suspects the ambush and flushes out His enemies with a question:

> "Is it lawful to heal on the Sabbath, or not?" (v. 3)

Earlier, the synagogue ruler had stated the official position of the Pharisees: healing is illegal on the Sabbath (see 13:14). Which of these religious experts would be willing to step forward and defend their law? After throwing down His challenge, Jesus hears a shuffling of feet and nervous coughs, but no one dares duel with Him over this issue. They know that God's law doesn't specifically forbid acts of compassion on the Sabbath, so they remain quiet (14:4a). Jesus breaks the silence and demonstrates God's official position on the question.

> And He took hold of him, and healed him, and sent him away. And He said to them, "Which one of you shall have a son or an ox fall into a well, and will not immediately pull him out on a Sabbath day?" And they could make no reply to this. (vv. 4b–6)

From Jesus' point of view, this man had fallen into a deep well of suffering. He was a son who needed saving, not a sinner who needed scolding. What kind of religion would leave him to languish in his pit because it was a "holy" day? The Pharisees couldn't answer Jesus for fear of revealing their own swollen hypocrisy.

Exhorting the Proud

In scene 2 of this domestic drama, the host relieves the awkward tension by calling everyone to the table. He and the Pharisees and lawyers lead the parade of invited guests into a spacious dining room, where a sumptuous banquet has been spread on a large U-shaped table. The bottom-center of the U is the seat of highest

2. William Hendriksen, *Exposition of the Gospel according to Luke*, from the New Testament Commentary series (Grand Rapids, Mich.: Baker Book House, 1978), p. 720.

honor, with the seats on its right and left the next highest, and so on in descending order to the ends.

As soon as the socialites enter the room, they start jockeying for the best seats. It's a grown-up version of musical chairs, and Jesus notices it. He sees the haughty glow in those who manage to grab the seats next to Pharisee So-and-So, as well as the sulky look on those who get bumped to the end, next to the kitchen. So He turns to the invited guests and serves them some wisdom in the form of a parable.

> "When you are invited by someone to a wedding feast, do not take the place of honor, lest someone more distinguished than you may have been invited by him, and he who invited you both shall come and say to you, 'Give place to this man,' and then in disgrace you proceed to occupy the last place. But when you are invited, go and recline at the last place, so that when the one who has invited you comes, he may say to you, 'Friend, move up higher'; then you will have honor in the sight of all who are at the table with you. For everyone who exalts himself shall be humbled, and he who humbles himself shall be exalted." (vv. 8–11)

You won't find many assertiveness-training seminars giving that advice, but it's been around a long time—since the days of Solomon (see Prov. 25:6–7). Today's wisdom says that getting ahead depends on how well we sell ourselves. Christ's teaching turns this self-promotion theory on its ear. His advice is, Be content with the back seat. Be happy with who you are and where you are. If God wants you in the front row, He'll move you there. And the honor will taste twice as sweet because you won't be expecting it.

Remembering the Needy

In the third scene, Jesus turns from the honor-seekers to address the one sitting in the "seat of honor," the host. Here is a man of influence. His guest lists include only the cream of society. But he's about to find out that God is not impressed.

> And He also went on to say to the one who had invited Him, "When you give a luncheon or a dinner, do not invite your friends or your brothers or

> your relatives or rich neighbors, lest they also invite you in return, and repayment come to you. But when you give a reception, invite the poor, the crippled, the lame, the blind, and you will be blessed, since they do not have the means to repay you; for you will be repaid at the resurrection of the righteous." (vv. 12–14)

We often give our hand in kindness to certain people because we're hoping they'll give us a hand up someday. We say to ourselves, "He can help my career," or "She can boost me to a higher social level." The voice of Jesus tells us to lift up those whom society has cast aside—the disabled, the hurting, the neglected. If we give to those who have nothing to give, God will reach into His vault of glistening treasures and reward us when we step into His kingdom.

Exposing the Uncommitted

This is hard truth for the people at the dinner party to swallow. Attempting to make Jesus' words more palatable, one of the guests opens the fourth scene with this exclamation, "Blessed is everyone who shall eat bread in the kingdom of God!" (v. 15). *The kingdom of God*—now that's a dinner party everyone wanted to attend. In the following parable, Jesus explains who will be the fortunate ones eating bread at God's kingdom banquet.

> But He said to him, "A certain man was giving a big dinner, and he invited many; and at the dinner hour he sent his slave to say to those who had been invited, 'Come; for everything is ready now.' But they all alike began to make excuses. The first one said to him, 'I have bought a piece of land and I need to go out and look at it; please consider me excused.' And another one said, 'I have bought five yoke of oxen, and I am going to try them out; please consider me excused.' And another one said, 'I have married a wife, and for that reason I cannot come.' And the slave came back and reported this to his master. Then the head of the household became angry and said to his slave, 'Go out at once into the streets and lanes of the city and bring in here the poor and crippled and blind and lame.'" (vv. 16–21)

God is the "master" who throws the feast; Jesus is the "slave" who delivers the message. Those on the guest list have known about the feast for a long time, for the invitations have already been sent. Yet when Christ announces the hour, they are preoccupied with other things.

One man is absorbed in his business dealings, another is anxious to try out his purchases, and a third is more interested in his new wife. So the Master opens the banquet to anyone who will follow Him—the trampled poor living on the streets; the downcast beggars on skid row; the blind, who stumble in the darkness. Then the Servant reports to the Master:

> "And the slave said, 'Master, what you commanded has been done, and still there is room.' And the master said to the slave, 'Go out into the highways and along the hedges, and compel them to come in, that my house may be filled. For I tell you, none of those men who were invited shall taste of my dinner.'" (vv. 22–24)

The Master's voice reverberates with the urgency of a ringing bell. Go! Cry out to everyone you see no matter who they are. *Compel* them to accept the invitation.

Christ is still crying out to the world to receive His offer of salvation and follow Him to the kingdom banquet. Many people make excuses, but plenty come—enough to fill God's house with everlasting joy.

Lessons Learned from a First-Century Meal

As the curtain closes on the scene at the Pharisee's house, we're left with the somber realization that none of those present will eat at God's table unless they choke down their pride and receive Christ's invitation. Did any of them do that? We're not told, but we assume they went on, unrepentant, with their dinner party.

So that *we* won't leave the party unchanged, let's take with us four truths from these four scenes.

First, *legalism blinds us and makes us shortsighted.* It blinds us to anyone who doesn't follow our lists of acceptable behavior. It makes us shortsighted to the needs of our world.

Second, *pride backfires and makes us selfish.* We start playing the childish game of who's-better-than-whom, and we end up losing.

Third, *compassion blesses us and makes us sensitive*. It helps us overlook the color of people's skin or the size of a person's wallet. We begin seeing others through Jesus' eyes.

Fourth, *salvation beckons us and makes us select*. With Christ, there is no middle ground. He makes us choose between the things of this world and the blessings of God's kingdom. God's celestial party is already being prepared. Will we be ready when the dinner bell rings?

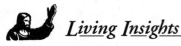

Living Insights — STUDY ONE

Have you ever played the grown-up version of musical chairs at work or at a party or a conference? The object is to maneuver yourself close to the person or group of people with the most influence. It's a subtle game with many strategies, all designed to move you to the top of the social or corporate ladder. After all, it's not what you know, but who you know . . . right?

Is there someone in a seat of honor that you're currently trying to get next to? What are you doing to edge your way up to him or her?

Is there someone you've been stepping over to get to this person?

What is Jesus' advice in Luke 14:7–11? How does this fit your situation?

It's tempting to try to maneuver ourselves into the position we want. But how much better to let our character do the talking and trust the Lord to advance us in His timing. What can you do to practice humility, particularly toward that person you've been stepping over?

Living Insights STUDY TWO

It's Saturday afternoon. Late. You have fifteen minutes to run into the store, bag a few items, and hurry home before your company arrives. You pull into the parking lot, crossing your fingers for a spot close to the front. The place is packed with cars, not an empty space anywhere . . . except three open slots right by the store entrance. Each of them is marked with a wheelchair painted in a blue circle.

As you drive by, you grumble, "These handicapped spaces are always empty. What a waste of good parking."

Finally, way out in the cracked and weedy part of the lot, you find a spot. It only takes a moment to hike to the entrance, but it's enough to raise beads of sweat on your forehead—and a flush of embarrassment when you see who has parked in one of the handicapped spaces. A man with braces on his legs struggles to lift himself out of his car. Adjusting his crutches, he slowly plants one foot in front of the other and hobbles into the store. A thought crosses your mind: *Imagine how hard it would have been for him to walk to the entrance from the back of the parking lot.*

Handicap parking spaces are one of the few places of honor that disabled people are given in our society. Yet, to our shame, we sometimes resent those and other allowances our government makes for the disabled. Jesus never grumbled about the lame or the blind. He gave them a special invitation to His kingdom party and encouraged us to make a place for them at our luncheons and dinners also (see vv. 13, 21).

Why do you think that Jesus had a special place in His heart for the disabled?

Are there any places of honor in your life for people with disabilities, whether physical or mental? What can you do to be more sensitive to their needs?

The next party you plan, be sure to include "the poor, the crippled, the lame, the blind" (v. 13) or anyone you know who doesn't have means to repay your kindness. And bring a little of God's kingdom into your home.

Chapter 15

EXACTING EXPECTATIONS

Luke 14:25–35

Seeking solace and relief from the pressures of his presidency, the great Abraham Lincoln was often known to slip away to the midweek service at New York Avenue Presbyterian Church. So as not to be disruptive, he would sit in the pastor's study to listen to the sermon, usually in the company of a young aide. On one particular night, the aide asked Lincoln how he liked the sermon.

> "I thought it was well thought through, powerfully delivered, and very eloquent," was the reply. "Then you thought it was a great sermon?" the young man continued. "No," said Lincoln, "it failed. It failed because Dr. Gurley did not ask us to do something great."[1]

When someone challenges us to do something great, it nearly always forces us to confront life-changing issues. That may feel uncomfortable, even agonizing. But it also feels invigorating, exciting, right. We yearn to hear the voice of God in our lives, for He not only asks great things, He expects great things.

He told Noah, "Build an ark!" He said to Moses, "Rescue My people!" To David he ordered, "Fight the giant"; to Elijah, "Prophesy a drought"; to Paul, "Come to Macedonia and preach."

In our passage in Luke, Jesus speaks with that same voice of authority, inspiring His soldiers to the highest level of devotion. Here we find some of the most demanding words in all the Bible. They're penetrating, exacting, and—frankly—tough. And they're for you, if you desire to be a disciple of Christ.

Clarifying a Necessary Distinction

Jesus' words in this passage are not meant for you, if you've

Portions of this chapter are adapted from "Cost of Discipleship . . . Consecration," in *Discipleship: Ministry Up Close and Personal*, coauthored by Lee Hough, from the Bible-teaching ministry of Charles R. Swindoll (Fullerton, Calif.: Insight for Living, 1990), pp. 35–41.

1. Bruce Larson, *What God Wants to Know: Finding Your Answers in God's Vital Questions* (New York, N. Y.: HarperCollinsPublishers, HarperSanFrancisco, 1993), pp. 46–47.

never received His gift of salvation. He doesn't expect people to follow His commands if they have not been born again. That would be like telling a dead person stretched out in a casket, "Up and at 'em! Get with it, soldier!" Christ has to breathe spiritual life into us before we have the capacity to obey. Conversion must come first, then consecration.

Once we receive Christ's gift, we begin to understand that He gave us life, not so that we might live for ourselves, but so that we might live for Him (see 2 Cor. 4:15). Exactly what does it mean to live for Him? Jesus' followers were asking that question too. We can listen in on His answer in Luke 14.

Hearing Some Strong Exhortation

As we pick up the story, Jesus has resumed His travel schedule, slowly wending His way through village after village toward the city of Jerusalem. Along the way, He stops to preach to the multitudes that swarm around Him.

The Setting

Like bees to honey, Jesus' public ministry attracted a following so thick He could hardly brush the people away long enough to catch His breath (v. 25a).

In His great potpourri of followers mingled interested seekers, skeptics who didn't buy any of what Jesus said, and a large number of window shoppers—people who simply enjoyed looking, listening, and occasionally getting free food.

The Requirements

It is to this crowd of seekers, skeptics, and the "just looking" that Jesus turns and outlines the stringent prerequisites for being one of His disciples. Three times Christ thins the ranks of those following Him with the exacting terms for consecration. Let's find out what those terms are.

Personal Relationships. First, we're required to place our relationship with Christ above all others.

> "If anyone comes to Me, and does not hate his own father and mother and wife and children and brothers and sisters, yes, and even his own life, he cannot be My disciple." (v. 26)

Is Jesus asking us to violate the Ten Commandments and literally hate our families? No, He's saying that our love for Him must outshine all other loves, even the love we feel for our families. His statement in Matthew 10:37 makes this clear:

> He who loves father or mother more than Me is not worthy of Me; and he who loves son or daughter more than me is not worthy of Me.

When a non-Christian father, for instance, warns his daughter not to believe "that Christianity nonsense," she must make the agonizing choice between him and the Lord. Unless she can cut her ties and follow Christ, she cannot be His disciple. She can still love her father, but her loyalty must lie with Jesus.

No doubt this is too high a price for many in the crowd surrounding Jesus, so they begin to leave. But He doesn't reduce the cost of discipleship to lure them back. Instead, He raises it with the next term, which calls for an even deeper commitment to consecration.

Personal Goals and Desires. Second, we're required to crucify our personal goals and desires for the sake of Christ.

> "Whoever does not carry his own cross and come after Me cannot be My disciple." (v. 27)

Here Jesus invokes an explicit image that is familiar to everyone present—the image of convicted criminals stumbling up their hill of execution, carrying the timbers upon which they will be crucified. The cross is a symbol of death, of violent death shrouded in shame. Jesus is saying that to be His disciples, we must put to death that part of us which resists Him, the part that wants to go our own way and pursue our own ambitions. Like Jesus in the Garden of Gethsemane, we need to cry out to God:

> "Father, if Thou art willing, remove this cup from Me; yet not My will, but Thine be done." (22:42)

Can we ask you to examine this area of your heart right here and now? The following three questions will help you see whether you're living according to your way or Christ's:

- Have I honestly and objectively taken my life's goals and desires before the Lord for His final approval?
- Do my goals and desires honor Him rather than simply make me happy?

- Am I really willing to change them if He were to show me that I should?

Personal Possessions. The third requirement is that, along with our relationships and our self-made plans, we must also lay our possessions before Him.

> "So therefore, no one of you can be My disciple who does not give up all his own possessions." (v. 33)

Again, Jesus is not speaking in literal terms. He's not saying that His disciples aren't supposed to own anything: rather, that no possession is supposed to own a disciple. How often we become slaves to the material things we buy, whether homes, cars, or even clothes. These things are not wrong in themselves, it's only when they keep us from being freed up to follow Him that they infringe on Christ's rightful ownership of our lives.

The Reasons

To many people, Jesus' requirements for discipleship seem too strict and unyielding. Their natural response is to ask *why*? Why does discipleship have to be so exacting? Jesus uses two stories to explain why such terms are necessary.

> "For which one of you, when he wants to build a tower, does not first sit down and calculate the cost, to see if he has enough to complete it? Otherwise, when he has laid a foundation, and is not able to finish, all who observe it begin to ridicule him, saying, 'This man began to build and was not able to finish.' Or what king, when he sets out to meet another king in battle, will not first sit down and take counsel whether he is strong enough with ten thousand men to encounter the one coming against him with twenty thousand? Or else, while the other is still far away, he sends a delegation and asks terms of peace." (vv. 28–32)

In his book *Strengthening Your Grip*, Chuck Swindoll explains that it is Jesus who is the builder and the king in the stories, not us.

> *We* are not told to count the cost. . . . Who, in the two stories, counts the cost? Well, the one in charge of the building project does that. And the king, who

> is responsible for the outcome of the battle, does that. Not the construction crews, not the fighting men. No, it's the one in charge.
>
> Obviously, it is the Lord Himself whom Jesus has in mind.[2]

Christ knows what it will take to build His kingdom; He knows the magnitude of the task and sees the relentlessness of the enemy. He knows the kind of commitment it will take to get the job done, and He's looking for the kinds of people who can rise to the challenge.

The Analogy

Jesus uses a natural preservative—salt—to crystallize His teaching and its importance in the minds of the people.

> "Therefore, salt is good; but if even salt has become tasteless, with what will it be seasoned? It is useless either for the soil or for the manure pile; it is thrown out. He who has ears to hear, let him hear." (vv. 34–35)

If we gloss over Christ's terms for discipleship, we lose our Christlike essence. We become bland Christians, providing neither the church nor the world the taste of Jesus that they crave. We become useless. God didn't create us just to fill pew space on Sunday mornings. He has great mountains for us to climb, great towers to build, great spiritual kingdoms to vanquish. But we must be willing to accept His challenge.

Responding to These Expectations

What must we do? To put it bluntly, we have to *stop indulging our laziness*. God didn't put us here to sip lemonade under a shade tree and watch the world go by. We have a job to do, a divine mission to accomplish. No commander ships his troops into enemy territory for a sightseeing cruise. Neither does Christ send us into Satan's domain to gather wildflowers. We need to find out where the action is, roll up our sleeves, and get involved.

Second, we need to *start demonstrating our devotion*. Saying we're disciples of Christ is like saying we sing like Pavarotti—no one

2. Charles R. Swindoll, *Strengthening Your Grip: Essentials in an Aimless World* (Dallas, Tex.: Word Publishing, 1982), pp. 122-23.

believes us until we open our mouths. Our devotion to Christ will show itself in our actions, as we surrender our relationships, our goals and desires, and our possessions to Him. Christ never said that being His disciple would be easy. He asks us to do something great. What will be our answer?

Living Insights — STUDY ONE

Jesus said that "no one of you can be My disciple who does not give up all his own possessions" (v. 33). Is there any more poignant example of discipleship than Abraham?

What God asked Abraham to give up stops the heart of any parent . . . his son Isaac (see Gen. 22:1–2). No more precious pearl lay in the vault of Abraham's heart than Isaac. He was Abraham's life, his future, his supreme joy. Abraham's herds of sheep and his vast wealth were mere baubles in comparison. He would rather have sacrificed them all, but God wanted Isaac. Only in that kind of obedience could the Lord be sure that Abraham was completely His.

You recall the story. In unwavering obedience, Abraham places his son on the altar. Trembling, determined, he raises his knife to plunge it into Isaac's heart. And then the voice of God stops Him. In his book *The Pursuit of God*, A. W. Tozer underscores the significance of this event:

> The old man of God lifted his head to respond to the Voice, and stood there on the mount strong and pure and grand, a man marked out by the Lord for special treatment, a friend and favorite of the Most High. Now he was a man wholly surrendered, a man utterly obedient, a man who possessed nothing. . . .
>
> . . . Yet was not this poor man rich? Everything he had owned before was his still to enjoy: sheep, camels, herds, and goods of every sort. He had also his wife and his friends, and best of all he had his son Isaac safe by his side. He had everything, *but he possessed nothing*. There is the spiritual secret. . . .
>
> After that bitter and blessed experience I think the words "my" and "mine" never had again the

> same meaning for Abraham. The sense of possession which they connote was gone from his heart. *Things* had been cast out forever.[3]

We may have many things—furniture, cars, a house—but if we're Christ's disciples, we must possess nothing. Everything goes on the altar, even our most cherished pearls.

Have you given up your possessions to the Lord? In your mind, follow Abraham to his altar on that windswept hill. Empty your storehouse of treasures and place them all before the Lord. What are the prizes you offer Him?

At first, we feel terrible pain, as did Abraham. But then we sense the Lord's presence, and our hands, now empty, reach out to Him. Whether He takes our offering or gives it back again, it doesn't matter now. Our security is in Him alone, and we know that He will provide.

Living Insights STUDY TWO

Jesus said, "You are My friends, if you do what I command you" (John 15:14). He asks a lot of us, but He has done a lot for us, so we announce, "Lord, I will gladly do whatever You say." Until . . .

- the parent we adore needs our signature to finalize a less-than-legal business deal.
- our boss hands us the promotion of our dreams, as long as we agree to compromise a few family priorities.
- we finally find the person we want to marry, but they're not a Christian.

3. A. W. Tozer, *The Pursuit of God* (Harrisburg, Penn.: Christian Publications, 1948), pp. 27–28.

Putting Christ first isn't easy. It may mean standing up to the dearest person in your life. It may mean passing up a golden opportunity. It may mean pushing aside a deep desire.

What sacrifices will you have to make in order to fulfill Christ's terms of discipleship . . .

. . . concerning your personal relationships?

. . . concerning your goals?

. . . concerning your desires?

Are you willing to lift these crosses to your shoulder and follow the Lord (Luke 14:27)?

Jesus knew that without His cross there could be no kingdom. Similarly, without our consecration, we can't participate in building His kingdom. The task is great, but the rewards are greater—greater than any earthly praise or pleasure. Ask Him for the strength to carry your cross and not settle for anything less than His kingdom.

Chapter 16

HOW TO MAKE THE ANGELS LAUGH

Luke 15:1–10

Sam is a carousing ex-baseball player who had his day in the big leagues but boozed away any hopes of stardom. Diane serves cocktails but dreams of living in a world of literature and fine art. Carla is a single mom, muscling her way through life on a waitress' salary. Rebecca's one goal was to marry a rich man. But, in the end, she settles for a plumber and a chance at love.

Then there's big Norm, who would rather be swigging beers with the boys than going home to his wife. His buddy Cliff is a mail carrier who delivers little besides talk. And Frazier is a troubled psychiatrist in a rocky marriage, with few real answers for life's problems.

These are the characters of the TV show *Cheers*. Everywhere we go, we see people like them. They are the bar crowd, needy people thirsting for a taste of hope and happiness, for fellowship over a drink or two, for a place of refuge where everybody knows your name.

To be painfully honest, most Christians are completely out of touch with this crowd, because their coarse ways grate like sandpaper against "polished" Christian lifestyles. But Jesus could see beneath the rough exterior of the Sams and Carlas and Norms of His day. He loved them. And they could talk to Him openly and find real answers. Jesus had a style that attracted lost souls and shattered the Pharisaic mold of what defined spirituality—many called His style revolutionary.

Jesus' Revolutionary Style

Jesus grew up in the remote and irreverent town of Nazareth. For thirty years, He worked with His hands as a carpenter. When He launched His ministry, He chose calloused fishermen and a crooked tax collector for His companions. While He chastised "good" people who sold religious products at the temple (John 2:13–16), He publicly defended an adulteress. He angrily denounced the venerated Pharisees as "blind guides" and "hypocrites" and refused to play by their pious rules. At the same time, He enjoyed rubbing elbows with the unseemly people of the world, so much that He was chided as a "gluttonous man, and a drunkard, a friend of tax-gatherers and sinners!" (Luke 7:34).

Jesus' actions demonstrated that He was a radical, and His words proved it. In a society built on legalism, He preached, "Don't judge one another." At a time of unrest and uncertainty, He said, "Don't worry." In a community where people trumpeted their holiness, He warned, "Don't show off." In a world of hate and war, He taught, "Forgive your enemies."

He advised the upper crust to invite the poor and the disabled to their society parties. He told leaders to serve, rather than be served. Instead of cultivating His popularity, He thinned the adulating crowds with hard sayings and exacting terms of discipleship. He was no ordinary religious man.

A Classic Case in Point

That is why the people flocked to see Him. Out of the taverns and up from the cellars they came. From back-alley hideouts, smoke-filled offices, and perfumed parlors; from gutters and shanties, from penthouses and slum houses, "all the tax-gatherers and the sinners were coming near Him to listen to Him" (15:1).

The Setting

Who were these people? The same ones who would later fill Christ's church. People like the Corinthian believers, who had once been fornicators, idolaters, adulterers, effeminate, homosexuals, thieves, covetous, drunkards, revilers, and swindlers—people, in fact, like us (see 1 Cor. 6:9–11).

However, while the lost souls of Palestine were following Jesus' beacon of grace, the legalists were scowling in self-righteous indignation and trying to shut Him down:

> And both the Pharisees and the scribes began to grumble, saying, "This man receives sinners and eats with them." (Luke 15:2)

To them, receiving "sinners" was tantamount to inviting slop-covered pigs to wallow in your living room. William Barclay elaborates on their disgust for these people:

> The Pharisaic regulations laid it down, "When a man is one of the People of the Land, entrust no

> money to him, take no testimony from him, trust him with no secret, do not appoint him guardian of an orphan, do not make him the custodian of charitable funds, do not accompany him on a journey." A Pharisee was forbidden to be the guest of any such man or to have him as his guest. He was even forbidden, so far as possible, to have any business dealings with him. It was the deliberate Pharisaic aim to avoid every contact with the people who did not observe the petty details of the law. . . . They looked sadistically forward not to the saving but to the destruction of the sinner.[1]

Consumed with disdain, the Pharisees stepped on sinners and tossed them aside as trash. But Jesus picked them up and cherished them as diamonds. Rather than punishing them for what they were, He rejoiced at what they could be.

In the following verses, He tells three stories that give three glimpses of grace—three never-seen-before views of what happens in heaven when one wayward sinner finds home.

The Stories

The first story is of the lost sheep (vv. 3–7); the second, of the lost coin (vv. 8–10); and the third, of the lost son (vv. 11–32). Let's examine the first two stories now and save the last one for the next chapter.

The Lost Sheep. For this story, Jesus invites us into the craggy hillsides and steep valleys that carve out the landscape of Palestine. This is the wild domain of the shepherd, who must always be watching for straying sheep. Jesus begins,

> "What man among you, if he has a hundred sheep and has lost one of them, does not leave the ninety-nine in the open pasture, and go after the one which is lost, until he finds it?" (v. 4)

Outside the shepherd's protection and the security of the flock, the lost sheep will certainly die. Wild animals will find it easy prey and quickly tear it to pieces. So he must hurry. He tracks the

1. William Barclay, *The Gospel of Luke*, rev. ed., The Daily Study Bible Series (Philadelphia, Pa.: Westminster Press, 1975), pp. 199–200.

frightened sheep through thick brambles and up rocky embankments. His pursuit is relentless. Finally, he hears the faint, woeful bleating of his lamb, still alive but wounded and half-starved. The shepherd rushes to its side and, with a swing of his strong arms, he hoists the animal and "lays it on his shoulders" (v. 5). Then all the way home, he scolds the sheep, right? "Look at the trouble you caused. How many times have I told you not to wander? . . ." No way!

> "And when he comes home, he calls together his friends and his neighbors, saying to them, 'Rejoice with me, for I have found my sheep which was lost!'" (v. 6)

This parable is not really about lost sheep, is it? It's about lost people. With masterful skill, Jesus draws both a comforting lesson for the crowd and a convicting one for the Pharisees.

> "I tell you that in the same way, there will be more joy in heaven over one sinner who repents, than over ninety-nine righteous persons who need no repentance." (v. 7)

What sets off the fireworks in heaven? Ninety-nine legalists completing the ninety-ninth requirement on their Sabbath checklist? Yawn. One prostitute weeping at the feet of Jesus or one dying criminal gasping, "Jesus, remember me when You come in Your kingdom" (23:42)—that's what lights the sky in heaven.

The Lost Coin. In the next verses, Jesus brings us back to earth for another story. This time, He takes us into an ordinary first-century home.

> "Or what woman, if she has ten silver coins and loses one coin, does not light a lamp and sweep the house and search carefully until she finds it?" (15:8)

She still has nine other coins, so why does she worry about this one? Because the coin is valuable; it is a *drachma*, worth about one day's wages.

Her mind spins, *Where could that coin be?* She tries every method she can think of to find the precious item. She lights an oil lamp. She sweeps the dirt floor, starting in the far corner and slowly working her way through the room. She searches through pockets and fishes behind furniture. She gets on her hands and knees and scours every inch of that house. Finally . . . "There it is!"

> "And when she has found it, she calls together her friends and neighbors, saying, 'Rejoice with me, for I have found the coin which I had lost!' In the same way, I tell you, there is joy in the presence of the angels of God over one sinner who repents." (vv. 9–10)

Remember who Jesus is addressing: "the tax-gatherers and sinners" who came to listen to Him (15:1). They are the lost sheep that Christ seeks and rescues. They are the precious coins whom He finds by turning the house inside out. And they are the children of the earth whose repentance causes the angels to ring the bells of heaven and fill God's creation with enough laughter to send the stars shooting into space.

Some Suggestions to Saints about Sinners

Do you see the unsaved people of your world the same way heaven sees them? Think of the overwhelming burden of guilt they carry. Think of their hopelessness when a loved one dies. Desperately, they search for love and meaning in life, yet everything they cling to becomes sand between their fingers. They are lost. But you can help them get found.

First, *stay in touch*. We need non-Christians as much as they need us. We need their honesty and their questions to help us be more authentic in our faith, and we need their ability to see through our pious acts to help keep us real.

Second, *treat them well*. Christ said to forgive our enemies, not strike back at them. If their earthy lifestyle embarrasses or offends you, don't judge them. Love them instead.

Third, *be very patient*. God is at work in their hearts, but remember that they may need time to change.

Remember the button people used to wear? "Please be patient, God isn't finished with me yet." That's as true for non-Christians as it is for Christians. Let's offer them the same grace we so generously give to each other.

Get to know some of your neighbors in the bar crowd, and give them a chance to know you. More importantly, give them a chance to know Jesus. He's been looking for them, and He longs to bring them home.

Living Insights — STUDY ONE

It's Friday night at the corner tavern. The owner flips on the neon sign out front and punches a button on the stereo. The groggy room awakens slowly to the sultry rhythm as a few silent figures drift in from the cold and take their usual seats. These are the world's wanderers—the lost souls who, for the moment, have found a place of refuge.

In their book, *The Edge of Adventure,* Keith Miller and Bruce Larson contend that these people have a lot more in common with teetotaling churchgoers than we might think.

> The neighborhood bar is possibly the best counterfeit there is to the fellowship Christ wants to give his church. It's an imitation, dispensing liquor instead of grace, escape rather than reality, but it is a permissive, accepting, and inclusive fellowship. It is unshockable. It is democratic. You can tell people secrets and they usually don't tell others or even want to. The bar flourishes not because most people are alcoholics, but because God has put into the human heart the desire to know and be known, to love and be loved, and so many seek a counterfeit at the price of a few beers.[2]

It's a shame that so many people seek imitations when the real thing is right down the street in church. The human heart finds its home in Christ. He offers lost souls the love they're searching for, and His church can provide them the unshockable, inclusive, and accepting air they need to breathe.

What has been your attitude toward the lost lately? Do you offer people a fresh breeze of unshockable grace? What kind of atmosphere do you create?

2. Keith Miller and Bruce Larson, *The Edge of Adventure: An Experiment in Faith* (Waco, Tex.: Word Books, 1974), p. 156.

What qualities in Christ drew "sinners" to Him?

Pick one of those qualities and write down ways you can demonstrate that quality to the unsaved people you meet.

Living Insights STUDY TWO

Dusk is slowly creeping over the horizon, sending streaks of orange across the sky and a chill wind across the weary backs of a group of hikers.

"None of this territory looks familiar," one says, straining to recognize a tree or a boulder.

Another shivers, "We'd better find some shelter, or we're going to freeze out here."

Gathering their strength, they trudge up one more ridge, hoping for a better lookout. From the top, they spot a meadow and a collapsing shack. Stumbling down the hill, they reach the old, dilapidated structure. It's not home, but at least it's a place to spend the night.

◆

People all over the world are searching for the spiritual trail that will lead them home. Their hearts yearn for the place of security and warmth that only Christ can give. But all they find are the collapsing shelters that the world offers—a passionate relationship, a fast-track career, a new form of entertainment.

Spend a few moments in the hiking boots of a weary worldly traveler. What would it be like to be always searching without finding what your heart seeks?

Do you know someone who is lost in sin's wilderness? Who?

This person won't find God's trail unless someone hikes into the woods to guide him or her. Are you willing go? What will it take for you to reach your friend?

The search may be long and difficult, but take heart in knowing that Jesus has already been looking for your friend for years. He hasn't given up yet, and, as long as the person you love is still lost in the woods, He never will. And neither should you.

Chapter 17

TWO REBELS UNDER ONE ROOF

Luke 15:11–32

As Jesus journeyed across Palestine, He must have marveled at the impressive Jordan valley. Towering cliffs rose above the river's twisting course, which plunged to depths 1,200 feet below sea level. Unlike a canyon, this valley was not dug by the watery bulldozer of erosion. Instead, parallel faults in the earth's crust made the ground sink, forming a giant fissure ten miles wide.

In Luke 15:11–32, Jesus stands before another chasm—a gaping rift between the "sinners" on one side of Him and the "righteous" Pharisees on the other.

The first group were people of the street. They lived to please only themselves, pushing aside every moral standard that stood in their way. On the other ledge were the legalistic Pharisees. They were people of the synagogue. Living to please a religious system, they set up moral standards almost as fast as the libertines could knock them down.

Any common ground between the two groups had sunk to jagged depths. Yet, from Jesus' perspective, there was really no such division. All were brothers, and all were sinners. One group had committed what we might call *detestable* sins; the other, *respectable* sins. But both stood guilty before their heavenly Father.

Bridging the sheer cliffs on either side of Him, Jesus constructed a parable that "has been called the greatest short story in the world."[1] It's the story many of us know as the parable of the prodigal son, but it's really about *two* sons—one who rebelled outwardly and one who rebelled inwardly . . . and the father who loved them both.

Wayward Lad . . . Waiting Dad

As Jesus raises the curtain on His story, the younger son takes center stage.

1. William Barclay, *The Gospel of Luke*, rev. ed., The Daily Study Bible Series (Philadelphia, Pa.: Westminster Press, 1975), p. 204.

Scene 1: Home, yet Dissatisfied

This young man approaches his father with a blunt demand: "Father, give me the share of the estate that falls to me" (v. 12a).

According to Jewish law, the father could release the inheritance before his death. The older brother would receive a "double portion" (two-thirds of the estate, in this case), and the younger brother would get the remainder (see Deut. 21:17).

As the father "divide[s] his wealth between them"[2] (Luke 15:12b), he most likely peers into the face of his younger son. Where is the little boy who used to call him Daddy? A wild stallion stands before him now, champing at the bit and straining for his freedom. Knowing that his son must make his own choices but still wanting to protect him, the father probably uses the time left to speak heart-to-heart with his boy. But this is one son who is set in his course.

Scene 2: Gone, but Miserable

So, "not many days later," this younger son shoves his belongings into a pack, casts off the harness of childhood, and steps onto the road of high adventure (v. 13a). With pockets bulging and confidence brimming, he strides into the sunrise of a new and unbridled life.

As the boy disappears over the horizon, however, the father sadly watches his sun set. How can he keep from wondering whether his son is safe? Whether he is sick? Whether he'll remember his father's love?

The prodigal's journey leads him to a distant country, a land flowing with temptation's sweet milk and delectable honey. Settling into a bachelor apartment, the young man hangs his motto on the wall: Eat, Drink, and Be Merry. Right away he finds a pack of shallow friends who are eager to help him spend his money and drink his wine.

The young man's whirling dance with the Devil goes on for weeks, maybe months—as long as he can cover the tab. One day, however, the bill is higher than he can pay. He has "squandered his estate with loose living," Jesus says (v. 13b). His funds have run out and so have his friends. He is just beginning to understand the true cost of sin.

2. *Both* boys receive their portion—it's only fair. If the younger son gets his share, the older should get his also.

> "Now when he had spent everything, a severe famine occurred in that country, and he began to be in need. And he went and attached himself to one of the citizens of that country, and he sent him into his fields to feed swine. And he was longing to fill his stomach with the pods that the swine were eating, and no one was giving anything to him." (vv. 14–16)

For a Jew, no job could be worse than slopping pigs—animals that were unclean, according to the Law. Yet here he is, covered head to toe with the muck they wallow in. Is this his long-sought-after pot at the end of the rainbow? When his hunger pangs drive him to the husks the pigs are eating, he finally realizes the animal he has become.

> "But when he came to his senses, he said, 'How many of my father's hired men have more than enough bread, but I am dying here with hunger! I will get up and go to my father, and will say to him, "Father, I have sinned against heaven, and in your sight; I am no longer worthy to be called your son; make me as one of your hired men."'" (vv. 17–19)

It is the image of his father, not his house or friends, that comes to the prodigal's mind. He remembers his father's love—and the pain in his eyes when he left home. His pangs of guilt begin to overtake his pangs of hunger. He understands now that he is the foolish son who brings "grief to his father, And bitterness to her who bore him" (Prov. 17:25). He is not worthy to be his father's son; the best he can hope for is to be his father's slave.

So he picks himself up and begins the long journey home.

Scene 3: Returned and Repentant

Every day since his son left, the father has paused from his work to gaze down the road, hoping this would be the day his boy would return. Now, as he leans on his hoe and squints into the distance, he spies a haggard figure stumbling toward him. Jesus describes what happens:

> "While he was still a long way off, his father saw him, and felt compassion for him, and ran and embraced him, and kissed him. And the son said to him, 'Father, I have sinned against heaven and in

> your sight; I am no longer worthy to be called your son.'" (Luke 15:20b–21)

The father runs to him and smothers him in unrestrained kisses. He doesn't even allow the boy to finish his speech, he's so overcome with joy. His son has come home!

Scene 4: Forgiven and Restored

Not letting the boy out of his grasp, the father shouts to his slaves:

> "'Quickly bring out the best robe and put it on him, and put a ring on his hand and sandals on his feet; and bring the fattened calf, kill it, and let us eat and be merry; for this son of mine was dead, and has come to life again; he was lost, and has been found.' And they began to be merry." (vv. 22–24)

Author Ken Gire explains the significance of these four gestures from the father to his son:

> For the son's lost dignity, the father bestows on him a robe of honor. For his bare servant's feet, he puts on them the sandals of a son. For the hand that squandered an entire inheritance, he gives a signet ring that reinstates the son's position of authority in the family business. For his empty stomach, he hosts a feast fit for a king.
>
> A robe, a pair of sandals, a ring, a feast. Symbols not only of forgiveness but of restoration. Gifts of grace, lavished on the one who deserved them least.[3]

As Jesus pauses at this point in the story, we can imagine Him looking deeply into the eyes of the sinners and tax gatherers. They are the real prodigal sons and daughters. The Father's gifts of grace are theirs, if they will only come home.

Then Jesus turns to the Pharisees.

3. Ken Gire, *Instructive Moments with the Savior* (Grand Rapids, Mich.: Zondervan Publishing House, 1992), p. 58.

Resentful Brother . . . Insightful Father

So far in the story, the older son has been standing in the shadows of the younger son's spotlight. Now it's his turn to be center stage.

> "Now his older son was in the field, and when he came and approached the house, he heard music and dancing. And he summoned one of the servants and began inquiring what these things might be. And he said to him, 'Your brother has come, and your father has killed the fattened calf, because he has received him back safe and sound.' But he became angry, and was not willing to go in." (vv. 25–28a)

His is a quiet, seething, vengeful anger. In his own way, he is as much a rebel as his younger brother. His father, seeing him standing outside, comes to him with the same gracious spirit extended to the younger son. He begins "entreating him" to join the celebration (v. 28b), but the older son replies hotly:

> "'Look! For so many years *I* have been serving you, and *I* have never neglected a command of yours; and yet you have never given *me* a kid, that *I* might be merry with *my* friends; but when this son of yours came, who has devoured your wealth with harlots, you killed the fattened calf for him.'" (vv. 29–30, emphasis added)

"I," "me," "my." The pride in his heart pours forth like a bitter fountain. William Barclay observes the implications of his scornful attitude.

> 1. His attitude shows that his years of obedience to his father had been years of grim duty and not of loving service.
>
> 2. His attitude is one of utter lack of sympathy. He refers to the prodigal, not as *my brother* but as *your son*.[4]

4. Barclay, *The Gospel of Luke*, p. 206. Barclay also speculates that the older brother "had a peculiarly nasty mind. There is no mention of harlots until he mentions them. He, no doubt, suspected his brother of the sins he himself would have liked to commit."

While his brother was off breaking his father's law, the older son was keeping it to the letter. However, by neglecting to cultivate love in the soil of his heart, his obedience had hardened into legalism. To him, sin must be punished; forgiveness, earned; kindness, deserved; and repentance, proven.

Instead of blasting him for his hypocrisy, the father addresses him with a gentle hand on his shoulder. As Jesus formulates the final words of His story, we can imagine Him stretching out His arms to the Pharisees—the angry, rebellious older sons.

> "And he said to him, 'My child, you have always been with me, and all that is mine is yours. But we had to be merry and rejoice, for this brother of yours was dead and has begun to live, and was lost and has been found.'" (vv. 31–32)

Detestable Sin . . . Respectable Sin

The younger brother revealed his rebellious nature through loose living. The older brother acted out his rebellious nature quietly, through pride and intolerance. Society would call the younger brother profligate, wanton, and detestable. But the older brother society would call responsible, deserving, and respectable.

To God, though, they're both sinners . . . rebels . . . lost. Only the younger brother was found. The older brother? The story remains open.

Jesus has a lesson for each type of rebel. First, *detestable rebels must face the painful reality of their "insanity" before they can repent.* Jesus says that the prodigal "came to his senses" (v. 17). Sin is like a psychosis; it blocks us from thinking rationally. Too often, it's not until we have our faces in the pig slop that we snap out of our groggy state of mind and see what sin is doing to us. It takes great patience to wait for a prodigal to sink to that point. And it takes God's grace to receive them back with open arms.

Second, *respectable rebels must face the awful ugliness of their pride before they can repent.* That's what makes it so difficult for Pharisees. Their arrogance prevents them from admitting their egotism! It takes courage to confront an "older brother," and it takes love to forgive them when they finally shed their pride and join the party.

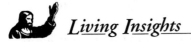

Living Insights STUDY ONE

Do you remember the Sirens in Greek mythology? Half bird, half woman, they lured sailors to destruction by the sweetness of their songs.

Temptation is like those mythical Sirens. Calling to us with a delightful, hypnotic voice, it promises pleasures beyond our most fantastic dreams. Though others shout out warnings, we're so intoxicated with its sweet harmonies that we hear nothing else. So we set our course toward sin, until, with a horrible crash, our ship slams into the rocks. Again and again, pounding waves throw us against sin's jagged edges until we're torn apart.

That is what happened to the prodigal son. And that is what happens in millions of lives every single day.

What sweet song does temptation sing to you?

What price do you pay when you listen?

The prodigal came to his senses by realizing what he was missing back home. What are you missing?

What will it take for you to get off and stay off the rocks?

◆

Not an easy question, is it? The answer may be as simple as repenting and returning to the welcoming arms of your heavenly Father. Or you may need some help. The Greek hero Odysseus had himself tied to the mast so he would not succumb to the Sirens' tantalizing song and steer his ship toward destruction.

Whatever it takes, even if it means sharing your struggles with someone you love, we urge you to do it. There's more to life than getting beat up on the rocks . . . or living in a pigsty.

Living Insights — STUDY TWO

If you were to cast yourself in Jesus' parable, which role would fit you better: the younger brother or the older one?

Since I'm asking the question, I suppose I should answer first. I'm usually not one to cast off all restraints and indulge in a worldly spree. But I am the type to criticize those who do. I tend to judge others by things like church attendance and religious deeds. So I see myself as the older brother, standing outside the party, measuring my worth against the people inside, and sulking because no one's throwing a party for me.

Whew! It feels better to have that off my chest. Would you like to take a turn?

Based on what the father told his sons in Jesus' story, let's try to hear what our heavenly Father would tell us. I think He would gently remind me to take my eyes off myself and soften my crusty legalism with a little love. What do you think He would say to you?

God's grace makes us want to celebrate, doesn't it? Whether we're more prodigal or more critical, let's determine not to stay away from the Father too long. He's throwing a party, and we don't want to miss one minute of it.

Chapter 18

WHAT'S AT THE CORE OF YOUR LIFE?

Luke 16:1–18

It's tough to live a focused life. From every direction, something or someone clamors for our attention. A distraction draws our eyes and the next thing we know, we've swerved off the road and headed down another detour.

One Chicago youth pastor came up with a clever way to keep his group on track. Concerned that the balmy beaches of Florida—the site of their upcoming evangelism trip—would lure the teens from their purpose, he fashioned a cross from two pieces of lumber. Just before they climbed on the bus, he showed it to the group.

"I want all of you to remember that the whole purpose of our going is to glorify the name of Christ, to lift up the Cross—the message of the Cross, the emphasis of the Cross, the Christ of the Cross," he announced. "So we're going to take this cross wherever we go."

The teenagers looked at one another, a little unsure of his plan. But they agreed to do it and dragged the cross on the bus. It banged back and forth in the aisle all the way to Florida. It went with them into restaurants. It stayed overnight where they stayed overnight. It stood in the sand while they ministered on the beach.

At first, lugging the cross around embarrassed the kids. But later, it became a point of identification. That cross was a constant, silent reminder of who they were and why they had come. They eventually regarded carrying it as an honor and privilege.

The night before they went home, the youth leader handed out two nails to each of the kids. He told them that if they wanted to commit themselves to what the cross stood for, then they could hammer one nail into it and keep the other with them. One by one, the teens drove their nail into the cross.

About fifteen years later, one fellow—now a stockbroker—called the youth leader. He told him that he still keeps that nail with him in his desk drawer. Whenever he loses his sense of focus, he looks for the nail and remembers the cross on that beach in Florida. It reminds him of what is at the core of his life—his commitment to Jesus Christ.

Where God Looks

What is at the core of your life? If you could take a surgeon's scalpel to the layers of activities and preoccupations and dig down to the very center of your soul, what would you find?

God's eyes slice through those layers with a single glance. As 1 Samuel 16:7 tells us, "God sees not as man sees, for man looks at the outward appearance, but the Lord looks at the heart."

Are the treasures He's given you being displayed proudly and usefully, or are they still in their boxes in a corner, making room for the world's wealth? Does He find the raw materials for building His kingdom or the blueprints to your own kingdom spread out and dominating the space? What does He see enthroned in your inner chamber, *His* cross, or *your* passion for power?

How We Live

It's not always easy to know the answer to those questions. Our hearts are mysterious territory, even to ourselves (see Prov. 20:5). Jesus, however, has given us a spiritual scope through which we can peer into the hidden places of our lives: money.

Surprised? Actually, the way we handle our finances provides a highly accurate view of our hearts, because our spending patterns reveal a great deal about our priorities.

Jesus' story about a crooked accountant memorably illustrates this principle.

> "There was a certain rich man who had a steward, and this steward was reported to him as squandering his possessions. And he called him and said to him, 'What is this I hear about you? Give an account of your stewardship, for you can no longer be steward.'" (Luke 16:1–2)

Knowing his days at this job are numbered, the accountant says to himself,

> "'What shall I do, since my master is taking the stewardship away from me? I am not strong enough to dig; I am ashamed to beg. I know what I shall do, so that when I am removed from the stewardship, they will receive me into their homes.'" (vv. 3–4)

He concocts a scheme to juggle the books one last time, hoping to win some friends who can help him later.

> "And he summoned each one of his master's debtors, and he began saying to the first, 'How much do you owe my master?' And he said, 'A hundred measures of oil.' And he said to him, 'Take your bill, and sit down quickly and write fifty.' Then he said to another, 'And how much do you owe?' And he said, 'A hundred measures of wheat.' He said to him, 'Take your bill, and write eighty.'" (vv. 5–7)

If you were the master, wouldn't you feel like you'd been stabbed in the back and now had the knife twisted? Here's another surprise:

> "And his master praised the unrighteous steward because he had acted shrewdly; for the sons of this age are more shrewd in relation to their own kind than the sons of light." (v. 8)

Amazing! Instead of blasting the accountant, the master tips his hat to him in admiration of his quick and clever thinking.

This story probably won't find its way into a business ethics textbook. All the characters—the master, the accountant, the debtors—are unscrupulous rascals. Out of this parable about bad people, however, emerge at least three good lessons.

First, *pursue wisdom and goodness with urgency.* Although the accountant pursued corrupt and selfish goals, he did so with urgency and foresight. In that sense, the "sons of this age" outshine us, "the sons of light" (v. 8). William Barclay explains:

> If only the Christian was as eager and ingenious in his attempt to attain goodness as the man of the world is in his attempt to attain money and comfort, he would be a much better man.[1]

In verse 9, Jesus shows us a specific way we can pursue wisdom and goodness:

> "And I say to you, make friends for yourselves by means of the mammon of unrighteousness; that

1. William Barclay, *The Gospel of Luke*, rev. ed., The Daily Study Bible Series (Philadelphia, Pa.: Westminster Press, 1975), p. 208.

when it fails, they may receive you into the eternal dwellings."[2]

Second, *pay more attention to being faithful than becoming famous*. Jesus draws out this lesson in verses 10–12:

> "He who is faithful in a very little thing is faithful also in much; and he who is unrighteous in a very little thing is unrighteous also in much. If therefore you have not been faithful in the use of unrighteous mammon, who will entrust the true riches to you? And if you have not been faithful in the use of that which is another's, who will give you that which is your own?"

The truth of our lives is revealed more in little ways than in large ways. How we handle the little, unseen things, like money, demonstrates our real character. God is not impressed by how good we look but by who we are and whether we're living up to our purpose. Barclay even goes so far as to say that

> what you get in heaven depends on how you use the things of earth. What you will be given as your very own will depend on how you use the things of which you are only steward.[3]

Third, *make the Lord your full-time master.* We all serve someone or something; and Jesus would have us be extremely clear about what we bow to, because that will define our life.

> "No servant can serve two masters; for either he will hate the one, and love the other, or else he will hold to one, and despise the other. You cannot serve God and mammon." (v. 13)

We cannot have a weekday god—money—and a Sunday God. At the core of our lives, there is room for only one passion. We must choose which one we'll serve.

2. The phrase *by means of the mammon of unrighteousness* implies that "God's people should be alert to make use of what God has given them." And *make friends for yourselves* carries the idea of "helping those in need, who in the future will show their gratitude when they welcome their benefactors into heaven ('eternal dwellings'). In this way worldly wealth may be wisely used to gain eternal benefit." *The NIV Study Bible*, gen. ed. Kenneth Barker (Grand Rapids, Mich.: Zondervan Bible Publishers, 1985), Luke 16:9 footnote.

3. Barclay, *The Gospel of Luke*, p. 209.

What Really Matters

The Pharisees, who have also been listening to Jesus, professed a devotion to God, but really, they were "lovers of money" (v. 14a). And Jesus' teaching has been hitting them right where they feel it the most—their money bags. Rather than repent of their greed, however, "they were scoffing at Him" (v. 14b). So Jesus confronted them with their hypocrisy.

> And He said to them, "You are those who justify yourselves in the sight of men, but God knows your hearts; for that which is highly esteemed among men is detestable in the sight of God." (v. 15)

Their lengthy prayers and righteous deeds may have wowed the people, but they nauseated God. He knew that greed was at the core of their lives. Greed for power. Greed for money. Greed for the perks that went along with piety in those days.

To make matters worse, they justified their hypocrisy with Scripture! They bent God's Word to fit their proud lifestyles, adding their interpretations to what God had said and calling their opinions divine. However, God would no sooner allow people to alter His Word according to their sinful hearts than He would allow Scripture to pass away into oblivion—something that will never happen.

> "The Law and the Prophets were proclaimed until John; since then the gospel of the kingdom of God is preached, and everyone is forcing his way into it. But it is easier for heaven and earth to pass away than for one stroke of a letter of the Law to fail. Everyone who divorces his wife and marries another commits adultery; and he who marries one who is divorced from a husband commits adultery." (vv. 16–18)

The word *stroke* refers to a tiny serif at the end of a Hebrew letter. The Law—even down to the smallest lines of a letter—had been chiseled in stone, and no amount of theological filing would erase its meaning. For instance, one group of Pharisees, from the school of Hillel, attempted to rub out God's Word on marriage by teaching that a man could divorce his wife for practically any reason. William Barclay lists a few of their reasons:

> "If she spoiled a dish of food; if she spun in the street; if she talked to a strange man; if she was guilty

> of speaking disrespectfully of her husband's relations in his hearing; if she was a brawling woman," which was defined as a woman whose voice could be heard in the next house.[4]

What a ridiculous interpretation of God's law! But Christ uses it to highlight our human tendency to twist the rules to fit our liking.

Have you ever played a board game with a four-year-old? If so, you know they only want to follow the rules as long as they are winning. As soon as the spinner says to dump out their cherries, or the minute the card says to go back to the candy canes, the child becomes instantly inventive: "I know! We won't *use* the cards!" or, "We all get to have *two* spins!"

The Pharisees were just like that with the Bible. They wanted to be in the game, but they wanted to play it their own way—keeping the rules that suited them, even expanding on them dramatically.

To be honest, wouldn't we like to do the same? But if we are truly to follow Christ, we've got to focus on the Cross, not our own comfort. We've got to play by His rules and live by His standards, even where no one else sees . . . because that's where it counts the most.

Why It's Important

It may be tough, but we need to live a life marked by focus, integrity, and loyalty to Christ. Why?

- *Because there are so many voices of authority, we need to focus exclusive attention on what God has said.* We may be pulled in many directions, but if our focus is on God's Word, we'll be able to keep firmly to the narrow path.

- *Because there is every temptation to emphasize externals, we need to pay more attention to what isn't seen.* With the Spirit's help, we can focus more on the truly valuable and lasting things of life, like character and relationships.

- *Because serving two masters is an impossibility, we need to return to our one and only Lord.* We need the Cross, not hanging from our necks on gold-plated chains, but planted deeply in the hidden soil of our hearts.

4. Barclay, *The Gospel of Luke*, p. 212.

Living Insights — STUDY ONE

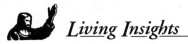

Not many of us have carried around a life-size cross like the youth group from Chicago did. But maybe we should try it sometime. Because crosses aren't meant to stay in churches. God wants us to carry them and their message wherever we go; He wants to make Christ the focus of our everyday lives.

How focused are you on Christ? Would those around you be able to tell that you are a Christian without your having to carry around a big cross?

Are you distracted by mammon? How?

Do you ever catch yourself adjusting Scripture to fit your lifestyle and desires? If so, in what areas?

Since lugging a cross around isn't very practical, what can you do to remind yourself of your purpose and keep your heart centered on Christ?

Why don't you take a few moments right now to refocus. Let the following prayer seep into your mind and penetrate your spirit.

Determine to keep your eyes on the Lord today and every day.

> *Lord, I would trust Thee completely; I would be altogether Thine; I would exalt Thee above all. I desire that I may feel no sense of possessing anything outside of Thee. I want constantly to be aware of Thy overshadowing Presence and to hear Thy speaking Voice. I long to live in restful sincerity of heart. I want to live so fully in the Spirit that all my thought may be as sweet incense ascending to Thee and every act of my life may be an act of worship. Therefore I pray in the words of Thy great servant of old, "I beseech Thee so for to cleanse the intent of mine heart with the unspeakable gift of Thy grace, that I may perfectly love Thee and worthily praise Thee." And all this I confidently believe Thou wilt grant me through the merits of Jesus Christ Thy Son. Amen.*[5]

Living Insights STUDY TWO

"Gold in California!"

In 1849, the news clanged like a bell across America, calling thousands of people to come west. The forty-niners tried every method they could think of to pull the glittering treasure out of nature's grasp. They burrowed deep into the earth. They sifted the sandy river beds. They eroded the hillsides with hydraulic cannons. Very few prospectors, though, accumulated much more than a sack full of crumbling dreams.

Spiritually speaking, like the hills of old California, Jesus' words contain riches beyond our wildest imaginations. Jesus, however, doesn't clutch His treasures as tightly as the earth guards its gold. His wealth is there for the taking and limitless in its supply for every prospector who comes to Him.

During our study, we've mined several passages in Luke and struck gold every time. Which nuggets are most precious to you? Under each of the following themes, write down one or two that gleam brightest to you.

5. A. W. Tozer, *The Pursuit of God* (Old Tappan, N.J.: Fleming H. Revell Co., n.d.), p. 128.

Jesus' Personal Encounters

(With Mary and Martha, the disciples, the stooped woman, etc.)

Jesus' Parables

(The rich fool, the faithful steward, the great supper, the lost sheep, the lost coin, the lost son, etc.)

Jesus' Confrontations with the Legalists

(Inner purity, the six woes, spiritual "table manners," the older son, lovers of money, etc.)

Jesus' Requirements for True Disciples

(Materialism, living vertically, preparing for the future, priorities, consecration, etc.)

Books for Probing Further

Jesus' words. Penetrating . . . encouraging . . . convicting. The challenges sheathed in His parables pierce to our heart's core, and we struggle to know how to respond to them—or even *if* we will respond.

What keeps us trying to live by Jesus' words? Perhaps we sense in them a greater reality than the one before our eyes, a greater call than all that tickles our ears. We find that we can't settle for the supposedly "easy" way, because our hearts concur with Peter:

> "Lord, to whom shall we go? You have words of eternal life." (John 6:68)

As you continue your quest to live out the eternal truths of Jesus' teachings, we encourage you to use the following resources. They can help you gain a broader, deeper understanding of Jesus' words—which alone are eternal, life giving, and able to transform your soul.

Blomberg, Craig L. *Interpreting the Parables*. Downers Grove, Ill.: InterVarsity Press, 1990. Comprehensive and thorough, this study is just the right tool for digging deep into Christ's parables.

Bock, Darrell L. *Luke*. The IVP New Testament Commentary Series. Downers Grove, Ill.: InterVarsity Press, 1994. This is an easy-to-read commentary by a Dallas Seminary professor who has spent years studying Luke's gospel.

Coleman, William L. *The Pharisees' Guide to Total Holiness*. Minneapolis, Minn.: Bethany House Publishers, 1977. This book ushers you into the world of the Pharisees and helps you understand why Jesus confronted them so relentlessly.

Gire, Ken. *Instructive Moments with the Savior: Learning to Hear*. Grand Rapids, Mich.: Zondervan Publishing House, 1992. This third volume in the author's excellent devotional series focuses on Jesus' teachings in Luke.

Lockyer, Herbert. *Everything Jesus Taught*. San Francisco, Calif.:

Harper and Row, Publishers, 1984. Organized topically, this book catalogues what Jesus said about Himself, the Father, the Spirit, sin, forgiveness, faith, money, prayer, and much more.

Pentecost, J. Dwight. *The Words and Works of Jesus Christ: A Study of the Life of Christ*. Grand Rapids, Mich.: Zondervan Publishing House, 1981. The author organizes Jesus' life around a kingdom theme and offers a clear, dispensational understanding of His teachings.

Wenham, David. *The Parables of Jesus*. Downers Grove, Ill.: InterVarsity Press, 1989. This book contains many keys for unlocking the mysteries of the parables, one of which is a valuable explanation of the kingdom of God.

Some of these books may be out of print and available only through a library. For those currently available, please contact your local Christian bookstore. Books by Charles R. Swindoll may be obtained through Insight for Living. IFL also offers some books by other authors—please note the ordering information that follows and contact the office that serves you.

NOTES

Notes

Notes

Notes

Notes

Ordering Information

Declaration of Something Mysterious

Cassette Tapes and Study Guide

This Bible study guide was designed to be used independently or in conjunction with the broadcast of Chuck Swindoll's taped messages which are listed below. If you would like to order cassette tapes or further copies of this study guide, please see the information given below and the order forms provided at the end of this guide.

		U.S.	Canada
DSM	**Study guide**	**$ 4.95 ea.**	$ 6.50 ea.
DSMCS	**Cassette series, includes all individual tapes, album cover, and one complimentary study guide**	**59.50**	69.50
DSM 1–9	**Individual cassettes, includes messages A and B**	**6.00 ea.**	7.48 ea.

The prices are subject to change without notice.

DSM 1-A: *Taming the Lion within Us*—Luke 10:38–42
B: *Lord, Teach Us to Pray*—Luke 11:1–13

DSM 2-A: *Storming Hellish Gates*—Luke 11:14–26
B: *How Jesus Handled Compliments and Crowds*—Luke 11:27–36

DSM 3-A: *Clean . . . from the Inside Out*—Luke 11:37–41
B: *Old Pharisees Never Die*—Luke 11:42–54

DSM 4-A: *Marching Orders for True Disciples*—Luke 12:1–12
B: *Testimony of a Fool*—Luke 12:13–21

DSM 5-A: *Vertical Living in a Horizontal World*—Luke 12:22–34
B: *Let's Be Ready for the Future*—Luke 12:35–48

DSM 6-A: *Let's Be Realistic about the Present*—Luke 12:49–59
B: *What a Difference Jesus Makes!*—Luke 13:1–17

DSM 7-A: *Straight Talk for Saints and Sinners*—Luke 13:18–35
B: *Spiritual Table Manners*—Luke 14:1–24

DSM 8-A: *Exacting Expectations*—Luke 14:25–35
B: *How to Make the Angels Laugh*—Luke 15:1–10

DSM 9-A: ***Two Rebels under One Roof***—Luke 15:11–32
B: ***What's at the Core of Your Life?***—Luke 16:1–18

How to Order by Phone or FAX

(Credit card orders only)

United States: 1-800-772-8888 from 7:00 A.M. to 4:30 P.M., Pacific time, Monday through Friday
FAX (714) 575-5496 anytime, day or night

Canada: 1-800-663-7639, Vancouver residents call (604) 596-2910 from 8:00 A.M. to 5:00 P.M., Pacific time, Monday through Friday
FAX (604) 596-2975 anytime, day or night

Australia and the South Pacific: (03) 9-872-4606 or FAX (03) 9-874-8890 from 8:00 A.M. to 5:00 P.M., Monday through Friday

---

Other International Locations: call the Ordering Services Department in the United States at (714) 575-5000 during the hours listed above.

How to Order by Mail

United States

- Mail to: Processing Services Department
  Insight for Living
  Post Office Box 69000
  Anaheim, CA 92817-0900
- Sales tax: California residents add 7.25%.
- Shipping and handling charges must be added to each order. See chart on order form for amount.
- Payment: personal checks, money orders, credit cards (Visa, MasterCard, Discover Card, and American Express). No invoices or COD orders available.
- $10 fee for *any* returned check.

Canada

- Mail to: Insight for Living Ministries
  Post Office Box 2510
  Vancouver, BC V6B 3W7
- Sales tax: please add 7% GST. British Columbia residents also add 7% sales tax (on tapes or cassette series).
- Shipping and handling charges must be added to each order. See chart

on order form for amount.

• Payment: personal cheques, money orders, credit cards (Visa, MasterCard). No invoices or COD orders available.

• Delivery: approximately four weeks.

Australia and the South Pacific

• Mail to: Insight for Living, Inc.
GPO Box 2823 EE
Melbourne, Victoria 3001, Australia

• Shipping: add 25% to the total order.

• Delivery: approximately four to six weeks.

• Payment: personal checks payable in Australian funds, international money orders, or credit cards (Visa, MasterCard, and BankCard).

Other International Locations

• Mail to: Processing Services Department
Insight for Living
Post Office Box 69000
Anaheim, CA 92817-0900

• Shipping and delivery time: please see chart that follows.

• Payment: personal checks payable in U.S. funds, international money orders, or credit cards (Visa, MasterCard, and American Express).

Type of Shipping	*Postage Cost*	*Delivery*
Surface	10% of total order*	6 to 10 weeks
Airmail	25% of total order*	under 6 weeks

**Use U.S. price as a base.*

Our Guarantee

Your complete satisfaction is our top priority here at Insight for Living. If you're not completely satisfied with anything you order, please return it for full credit, a refund, or a replacement, as *you* prefer.

Insight for Living Catalog

The Insight for Living catalog features study guides, tapes, and books by a variety of Christian authors. To obtain a free copy, call us at the numbers listed above.

Order Form
United States, Australia, and Other International Locations

(Canadian residents please use order form on reverse side.)

DSMCS represents the entire *Declaration of Something Mysterious* series in a special album cover, while DSM 1–9 are the individual tapes included in the series. DSM represents this study guide, should you desire to order additional copies.

DSM	**Study guide**	**$ 4.95 ea.**
DSMCS	**Cassette series, includes all individual tapes, album cover, and one complimentary study guide**	**59.50**
DSM 1–9	**Individual cassettes, includes messages A and B**	**6.00 ea.**

Product Code	Product Description	Quantity	Unit Price	Total
			$	$

Subtotal	
California Residents—Sales Tax *Add 7.25% of subtotal.*	
UPS ❏ First Class ❏ *Shipping and handling must be added. See chart for charges.*	
Non-United States Residents *Australia add 25%. All other locations: U.S. price plus 10% surface postage or 25% airmail.*	
Gift to Insight for Living *Tax-deductible in the United States.*	
Total Amount Due *Please do not send cash.*	$

Amount of Order	*First Class*	*UPS*
$ 7.50 and under	1.00	4.00
$ 7.51 to 12.50	1.50	4.25
$12.51 to 25.00	3.50	4.50
$25.01 to 35.00	4.50	4.75
$35.01 to 60.00	5.50	5.25
$60.00 and over	6.50	5.75

Fed Ex and Fourth Class are also available. Please call for details.

Prices are subject to change without notice.

Payment by: ❏ Check or money order payable to Insight for Living ❏ Credit card

(Circle one): Visa MasterCard Discover Card American Express BankCard (In Australia)

Number ____________________

Expiration Date __________ Signature ____________________

We cannot process your credit card purchase without your signature.

Name ____________________

Address ____________________

City ____________________ State __________

Zip Code __________ Country ____________________

Telephone (   ) ____________________ Radio Station ____ ____ ____ ____

If questions arise concerning your order, we may need to contact you.

Mail this order form to the Processing Services Department at one of these addresses:

Insight for Living
Post Office Box 69000, Anaheim, CA 92817-0900

Insight for Living, Inc.
GPO Box 2823 EE, Melbourne, VIC 3001, Australia

Order Form
Canadian Residents

(Residents of the United States, Australia, and other international locations, please use order form on reverse side.)

DSMCS represents the entire *Declaration of Something Mysterious* series in a special album cover, while DSM 1–9 are the individual tapes included in the series. DSM represents this study guide, should you desire to order additional copies.

DSM	**Study guide**	**$ 6.50 ea.**
DSMCS	**Cassette series, includes all individual tapes, album cover, and one complimentary study guide**	**69.50**
DSM 1–9	**Individual cassettes, includes messages A and B**	**7.48 ea.**

Product Code	Product Description	Quantity	Unit Price	Total
			$	$

Subtotal	
Add 7% GST	
British Columbia Residents *Add 7% sales tax on individual tapes or cassette series.*	
Shipping *Shipping and handling must be added. See chart for charges.*	
Gift to Insight for Living Ministries *Tax-deductible in Canada.*	
Total Amount Due *Please do not send cash.*	$

Amount of Order	*Canada Post*
Orders to $10.00	2.00
$10.01 to 30.00	3.50
$30.01 to 50.00	5.00
$50.01 to 99.99	7.00
$100 and over	Free

Loomis is also available. Please call for details.

Prices are subject to change without notice.

Payment by: ❑ Cheque or money order payable to Insight for Living Ministries
❑ Credit card

(Circle one): Visa MasterCard Number____________________

Expiration Date__________ Signature____________________

We cannot process your credit card purchase without your signature.

Name______________________________

Address______________________________

City____________________ Province__________

Postal Code____________ Country________________

Telephone (   )______________ Radio Station____ ____ ____ ____

If questions arise concerning your order, we may need to contact you.

Mail this order form to the Processing Services Department at the following address:

Insight for Living Ministries
Post Office Box 2510
Vancouver, BC, Canada V6B 3W7

Order Form

United States, Australia, and Other International Locations

(Canadian residents please use order form on reverse side.)

DSMCS represents the entire *Declaration of Something Mysterious* series in a special album cover, while DSM 1–9 are the individual tapes included in the series. DSM represents this study guide, should you desire to order additional copies.

DSM	**Study guide**	**$ 4.95 ea.**
DSMCS	**Cassette series, includes all individual tapes, album cover, and one complimentary study guide**	**59.50**
DSM 1–9	**Individual cassettes, includes messages A and B**	**6.00 ea.**

Product Code	Product Description	Quantity	Unit Price	Total
			$	$

Amount of Order	*First Class*	*UPS*
$ 7.50 and under	1.00	4.00
$ 7.51 to 12.50	1.50	4.25
$12.51 to 25.00	3.50	4.50
$25.01 to 35.00	4.50	4.75
$35.01 to 60.00	5.50	5.25
$60.00 and over	6.50	5.75

Fed Ex and Fourth Class are also available. Please call for details.

Subtotal	
California Residents—Sales Tax *Add 7.25% of subtotal.*	
UPS ❑ **First Class** ❑ *Shipping and handling must be added. See chart for charges.*	
Non-United States Residents *Australia add 25%. All other locations: U.S. price plus 10% surface postage or 25% airmail.*	
Gift to Insight for Living *Tax-deductible in the United States.*	
Total Amount Due *Please do not send cash.*	$

Prices are subject to change without notice.

Payment by: ❑ Check or money order payable to Insight for Living ❑ Credit card

(Circle one): Visa MasterCard Discover Card American Express BankCard (In Australia)

Number ______________________________

Expiration Date __________ Signature ______________________________

We cannot process your credit card purchase without your signature.

Name ______________________________

Address ______________________________

City ______________________________ State __________

Zip Code ______________ Country ______________________________

Telephone (   ) ______________________ Radio Station ____ ____ ____ ____

If questions arise concerning your order, we may need to contact you.

Mail this order form to the Processing Services Department at one of these addresses:

Insight for Living
Post Office Box 69000, Anaheim, CA 92817-0900

Insight for Living, Inc.
GPO Box 2823 EE, Melbourne, VIC 3001, Australia

Order Form
Canadian Residents

(Residents of the United States, Australia, and other international locations, please use order form on reverse side.)

DSMCS represents the entire *Declaration of Something Mysterious* series in a special album cover, while DSM 1–9 are the individual tapes included in the series. DSM represents this study guide, should you desire to order additional copies.

DSM	**Study guide**	**$ 6.50 ea.**
DSMCS	**Cassette series, includes all individual tapes, album cover, and one complimentary study guide**	**69.50**
DSM 1–9	**Individual cassettes, includes messages A and B**	**7.48 ea.**

Product Code	Product Description	Quantity	Unit Price	Total
			$	$

Amount of Order	*Canada Post*
Orders to $10.00	2.00
$10.01 to 30.00	3.50
$30.01 to 50.00	5.00
$50.01 to 99.99	7.00
$100 and over	Free

Loomis is also available. Please call for details.

Subtotal	
Add 7% GST	
British Columbia Residents *Add 7% sales tax on individual tapes or cassette series.*	
Shipping *Shipping and handling must be added. See chart for charges.*	
Gift to Insight for Living Ministries *Tax-deductible in Canada.*	
Total Amount Due *Please do not send cash.*	$

Prices are subject to change without notice.

Payment by: ❑ Cheque or money order payable to Insight for Living Ministries
❑ Credit card

(Circle one): Visa MasterCard Number ______________________________

Expiration Date __________ Signature ______________________________

We cannot process your credit card purchase without your signature.

Name ____

Address ____

City ______________________________ Province __________

Postal Code __________________ Country ______________________

Telephone (   ) ______________________ Radio Station ____ ____ ____ ____

If questions arise concerning your order, we may need to contact you.

Mail this order form to the Processing Services Department at the following address:

Insight for Living Ministries
Post Office Box 2510
Vancouver, BC, Canada V6B 3W7

CANADIAN COUNCIL OF CHRISTIAN CHARITIES CCCC FINANCIAL ACCOUNTABILITY

Order Form
United States, Australia, and Other International Locations

(Canadian residents please use order form on reverse side.)

DSMCS represents the entire *Declaration of Something Mysterious* series in a special album cover, while DSM 1–9 are the individual tapes included in the series. DSM represents this study guide, should you desire to order additional copies.

DSM	**Study guide**	**$ 4.95 ea.**
DSMCS	**Cassette series, includes all individual tapes, album cover, and one complimentary study guide**	**59.50**
DSM 1–9	**Individual cassettes, includes messages A and B**	**6.00 ea.**

Product Code	Product Description	Quantity	Unit Price	Total
			$	$

Amount of Order	*First Class*	*UPS*
$ 7.50 and under	1.00	4.00
$ 7.51 to 12.50	1.50	4.25
$12.51 to 25.00	3.50	4.50
$25.01 to 35.00	4.50	4.75
$35.01 to 60.00	5.50	5.25
$60.00 and over	6.50	5.75

Fed Ex and Fourth Class are also available. Please call for details.

Subtotal	
California Residents—Sales Tax *Add 7.25% of subtotal.*	
UPS ❑ First Class ❑ *Shipping and handling must be added. See chart for charges.*	
Non-United States Residents *Australia add 25%. All other locations: U.S. price plus 10% surface postage or 25% airmail.*	
Gift to Insight for Living *Tax-deductible in the United States.*	
Total Amount Due *Please do not send cash.*	$

Prices are subject to change without notice.

Payment by: ❑ Check or money order payable to Insight for Living ❑ Credit card

(Circle one): Visa MasterCard Discover Card American Express BankCard (In Australia)

Number ______________________

Expiration Date __________ Signature ______________________

We cannot process your credit card purchase without your signature.

Name ______________________

Address ______________________

City ______________________ State __________

Zip Code __________ Country ______________________

Telephone (   ) ______________ Radio Station ___ ___ ___ ___

If questions arise concerning your order, we may need to contact you.

Mail this order form to the Processing Services Department at one of these addresses:

Insight for Living
Post Office Box 69000, Anaheim, CA 92817-0900

Insight for Living, Inc.
GPO Box 2823 EE, Melbourne, VIC 3001, Australia

Order Form
Canadian Residents

(Residents of the United States, Australia, and other international locations, please use order form on reverse side.)

DSMCS represents the entire *Declaration of Something Mysterious* series in a special album cover, while DSM 1–9 are the individual tapes included in the series. DSM represents this study guide, should you desire to order additional copies.

DSM	**Study guide**	**$ 6.50 ea.**
DSMCS	**Cassette series, includes all individual tapes, album cover, and one complimentary study guide**	**69.50**
DSM 1–9	**Individual cassettes, includes messages A and B**	**7.48 ea.**

Product Code	Product Description	Quantity	Unit Price	Total
			$	$

Amount of Order	Canada Post
Orders to $10.00	2.00
$10.01 to 30.00	3.50
$30.01 to 50.00	5.00
$50.01 to 99.99	7.00
$100 and over	Free

Loomis is also available. Please call for details.

Subtotal	
Add 7% GST	
British Columbia Residents *Add 7% sales tax on individual tapes or cassette series.*	
Shipping *Shipping and handling must be added. See chart for charges.*	
Gift to Insight for Living Ministries *Tax-deductible in Canada.*	
Total Amount Due *Please do not send cash.*	$

Prices are subject to change without notice.

Payment by: ❑ Cheque or money order payable to Insight for Living Ministries
❑ Credit card

(Circle one): Visa MasterCard Number ____________________

Expiration Date __________ Signature ____________________
We cannot process your credit card purchase without your signature.

Name ____________________

Address ____________________

City ____________________ Province __________

Postal Code __________ Country ____________________

Telephone (   ) ____________________ Radio Station ___ ___ ___ ___
If questions arise concerning your order, we may need to contact you.

Mail this order form to the Processing Services Department at the following address:

Insight for Living Ministries
Post Office Box 2510
Vancouver, BC, Canada V6B 3W7

CANADIAN COUNCIL OF CHRISTIAN CHARITIES
CCCC
FINANCIAL ACCOUNTABILITY